what's wrong with

with
my plant?

hamlyn

what's wrong with my plant?

expert information at your fingertips

▶ Pests
▶ Diseases
▶ Common problems

Steven Bradley

First published in Great Britain in 2003 by
Hamlyn, a division of Octopus Publishing Group Ltd
2–4 Heron Quays, London E14 4JP

Distributed in the United States and Canada by
Sterling Publishing Co., Inc.
387 Park Avenue South, New York, NY 10016-8810

ISBN 0 600 60568 X

A CIP catalogue record for this book is available from
the British Library

Printed and bound in China

10 9 8 7 6 5 4 3 2 1

contents

introduction

Aah, the joys of the garden! A place where you can refresh your soul after a busy day, as you gaze on your even lawn, full flowerbeds, neat vegetable patch and laden fruit trees.

Oh yes? Chances are it's far more likely, as you walk around your carefully tended garden, that you will notice that this plant has holes in some of the leaves, that that one is a strange colour and that the one at the back is wilting slightly. It's not your fault: you have simply (and unwittingly) been preparing a gourmet banquet for the multitude of organisms that depend on plants for life.

If it's any consolation, these creatures, fungi and bacteria also feed and dwell on plants in the wild, but gardens, which are usually fairly sheltered and contain a range of healthy host plants, offer them better conditions. Given the rate at which some of these unwelcome invaders reproduce, it is hardly surprising that these attacks can, sometimes, be overwhelming.

Dealing successfully with any attack depends on vigilance (to spot the attack in the first place), on speed of response (to deal with it before it can become a threat to the plant) and on persistence (one treatment may not be enough to deal with all the generations of a pest that are present on the plant). Success often comes with experience, and there is really no substitute for getting to know your own plants – what colour they are when they are healthy, how they grow and what their various stages of growth look like. When you know what healthy specimens look like, when a plant becomes discoloured or its growth is distorted you will notice straight away and respond promptly with a treatment. Until you reach that stage, however, it is easy to be disheartened by ravaged crops and poor flowers. The best substitute for an expert gardener is a really good book that describes what you are seeing, tells you what the possible causes are and offers advice on alternative treatments according to how you choose to garden.

You don't need to fill your garage or garden shed with chemicals to treat your plants – they can't read, so your clematis will be none the wiser if you use a rose fungicide to treat its mildew. Changes in the way chemicals are authorized and regulated mean that some familiar names have disappeared from the shelves of garden centres and new ones are appearing. In any case, garden chemicals are constantly being reformulated and improved by manufacturers, so in this book they are referred to by their active ingredient (which is always shown on the label of the product) because this is less likely to alter. Many of the newer treatments are based on natural fatty acids, rather than on man-made

We tend to take healthy plants for granted, only reacting when symptoms appear, rather than checking plants on a regular basis.

chemicals, and they are proving to be just as effective and without having any lasting side-effects. This is better for the environment and means that the organic gardener is at last being offered an effective arsenal with which to protect both cropping and ornamental plants.

This book aims to give you a comprehensive insight into what could be attacking your plants and tell you how to deal with it quickly and effectively. Whether you are a novice gardener or have years of experience, you are just as likely to find something attacking your plants that you have never come across before. Climate change means that pests and diseases are migrating to areas that have previously been inhospitable for them, and a general reduction in cold weather means that insect populations are no longer killed off in winter. Indeed, some insects are remaining active throughout the winter months, so that by the time spring brings warmer weather, the populations are such that they can become epidemic within weeks.

The main key to success, if you do find an attack being waged on your plants, is identification. Some symptoms can have different causes – yellow mottling on leaves may, for example, be caused by greenhouse red spider mite, a virus or a mineral deficiency. Accurately identifying which is responsible will allow you to treat the problem in its early stages. You can waste time and money applying the wrong treatment, and the delay might even cost you the plant itself.

We will tackle the problems from both sides, explaining the different types of attacker (and the damage they can inflict) and also working back from the damage you are looking at (trouble-shooting to identify the likely cause). This is the book to take into the garden when you see a problem. A small hand lens will help make identification of tiny pests easier, but in most cases the diagnosis will be possible without one. Your garden will never be free of unwanted invaders, but at least now you will know how to deal with them.

what is a plant pest?

'Pest' is the name given to a living creature that either feeds on or harms a plant in some way. The damage may range from the occasional nibbling of leaves to killing the plant. Larger pests, such as slugs, snails and rabbits, are well-known plant chewers and are easy to see (or, at least, the injury they cause is readily identifiable). Others are much smaller, and this latter group includes the largest category: insects or their close relatives. These are not always recognizable as insects when they are seen on the plant, because many feed on plants before they reach their adult stage – caterpillars, grubs and, especially, slugworms are hard to associate with their adult forms.

A pest's feeding habit will determine how it damages a plant and what part of the plant is affected, although sometimes the entire plant is harmed, especially if a large population is living on a single specimen. Pests feed in various ways:

- scraping away surface tissue – e.g., slugs and snails
- sucking sap – e.g., aphids
- biting and chewing – e.g., caterpillars and sciarid flies (fungus gnats)
- mining through the foliage of plants – e.g., chrysanthemum miners
- tunnelling through stems and roots – e.g., goat moth (*Cossus cossus*) and wireworm (*Athous haemorrhoidalis* and *Agriotes* spp.)

Other pests will feed on fruits and seeds, with adults often laying their eggs close by so that the young have a feeding site as soon as they hatch.

Sometimes, as in the case of the oak-apple gall wasp (*Biorhiza pallida*), the pest will cause abnormal swollen growths (known as galls), when localized feeding causes distorted cell formation. They can also, as in the case of capsid bugs (*Lygus rugulipennis* and *Lygocoris pabulinus*), cause inadvertent damage by injecting toxins into the plant that lead to localized tissue death.

Other pests damage plants indirectly by transmitting bacterial, fungal or viral diseases. Birds, for example, are believed to play a part in the transfer of the fireblight bacterium to healthy plants, and the main spread of Dutch elm disease fungus is on the hairs on the legs of the elm bark beetle (*Scolytus* spp.). The peach-potato aphid (*Myzus persicae*) is notorious for the number of viruses it can transmit from infected to healthy plants.

Pests that feed on plant roots can also have a longer-term effect. The feeding wounds they create will often become the sites of primary infection for soil-borne bacteria or fungi, which would not normally enter the plant through healthy roots.

In some cases, the feeding site can be easily seen, even if the pest causing the

Bullfinches are very attractive birds with bright markings, but they can devastate fruit trees by eating their buds in a cold winter.

damage cannot. For example, the caterpillars of the so-called carpenter moths, such as the leopard moth (*Zeuzera pyrina*), leave piles of sawdust outside their feeding holes, and the sugary excrement (honeydew) left by insects, including aphids, coats the plant's leaves and encourages the development of sooty moulds over leaves and stems.

Some of the largest pests can quickly do real harm to plants. Deer and rabbits feed on plants, and grey squirrels and deer can strip the bark off trees and shrubs, causing death over large sections of the plant. However, some of this type of damage can be inadvertent – the large holes dug in lawns and borders by badgers and foxes, for instance, are the result of their search for food, such as chafer grubs, leatherjackets and worms, rather than an interest in the lawn itself. Perhaps the best (and most frustrating) example of this is the lawn devastated by moles as they search for earthworms, creating mole hills and undermining plants with their tunnelling. In this instance, the plants are damaged unwittingly as the moles have no particular interest in them as food.

In large numbers, caterpillars can defoliate plants within a few days of hatching.

what is a plant disease?

A plant disease is any pathological condition caused by other organisms, such as bacteria, fungi or viruses, that make the plant malfunction in some way and may lead to the death of the host plant. Sometimes the harmful organism is spread by a carrier, such as an aphid or eelworm (nematode), by bark beetles carrying Dutch elm fungus or water splashes dispersing bacterial spores. The pathogen is sometimes visible as a discoloration on the plant, as with silver leaf of plums and cherries. Leaf discoloration and distortion and wilting, stunted growth are typical symptoms of infection.

Fungi

Fungal diseases are the most common group of diseases to afflict plants, and it is believed that there are at least 100,000 species of fungus, although not all act as plant parasites. They are usually divided into three main categories, depending on their method of association with plants:

- obligate parasites must live on a live host – e.g., clubroot of brassicas – and although they will severely disrupt a plant's growth they rarely kill it, as the parasites would also kill themselves
- obligate saprophytes feed only on dead plant material and rarely represent a threat to healthy plants
- facultative parasites will live on dead or live plants – e.g., coral spot fungus,

which usually starts its life on dead shoots and gradually invades the living tissue, killing the host plant over a period of time and then feeding on the dead tissue

Bacteria

Bacteria that are harmful to plants are relatively rare – there are probably fewer than 2,000 species – although a few can have a devastating effect. The symptoms that these organisms produce vary considerably in appearance and severity, but the growth or health of the plant is almost always affected and, in severe attacks, the plant may even be killed. The rate of infection and the spread of the disease within the plant are affected by factors such as weather, growing conditions and the health of the host at the time of infection. For example, healthy plants may show signs of bacterial canker in the form of shot-hole symptoms, but the infection does not spread into the rest of the plant, so the small pieces of dead leaf simply fall away. These bacterial infections are worse when the surrounding atmosphere is warm and humid, favouring the rapid spread and development of the harmful organisms as they multiply at an alarming rate.

Viruses

Virus is a blanket term for a range of diseases, including mycoplasmas,

Some types of fungi can kill even the largest of trees, and in the case of Dutch elm disease, the damage they cause can completely change the landscape.

phytoplasmas, viroids and viruses themselves, that can have a devastating effect on plants. This group of pathogens have been described as the ultimate parasites because they need a host to develop and grow so that they become a part of their host, living in it rather than on it, as fungi and bacteria do. Unfortunately, this characteristic makes them almost impossible to treat and eradicate outside a well-equipped laboratory.

Viral diseases can be spread in a number of ways, but usually by means of the transfer of sap from infected hosts to clean, uninfected ones. In addition to the feeding action of sap-sucking insects, this can be caused by taking cuttings, budding and grafting, when knives and secateurs act as carriers and spread disease.

The typical symptoms of many viruses are stunted and distorted growth, leaf mottling and paler marking on flowers. Some roses may even develop green petals. The presence of an actual virus in a plant can be difficult to identify, however, because different plants can develop different symptoms even when they are infected with an identical virus.

Some fungal diseases will cause major disruption to a plant's natural growth, often culminating in strange swellings or gall-like injuries on the host.

what is a plant disorder?

A plant disorder is anything that cannot be classed as a pest or disease but that causes a malformation of growth or the death of a plant. Unless they are correctly diagnosed and treated, most plant problems can cause the death of the plant. It is a large group, which includes problems arising from:

- inadequate or erratic water supply
- inadequate or erratic food supply
- inappropriate light
- inappropriate temperature range
- unsuitable growing conditions
- unsuitable storage conditions
- unsatisfactory atmospheric conditions

Any of these factors, or a combination of several of them, may lead to a physiological disorder in the plant. What it is and how long it lasts will determine how harmful it is to a particular plant or group of plants.

Environmental problems

Any plant that lacks water, food or the appropriate environmental conditions for good growth may not necessarily appear unhealthy (unless it is directly compared with plants in perfect condition), but it will be far less resistant to attacks from pests or diseases.

The most common disorders are to do with water. Plants consist of about 90 per cent water and depend on it for all their functions, so a lack of it (drought, which causes the plant to wilt and, in extreme conditions, to die) or too much of it (waterlogging, which drives the oxygen out of the compost or soil in which the plant is growing) causes the roots to stop functioning, wither or rot and eventually die.

Environmental conditions have a strong influence on how well a plant can perform. Extreme temperature levels can create problems for plants at both ends of the scale. We are all familiar with frost damage to plants, but high temperatures can slow down growth as most plants are unable to perform many of the chemical processes essential to growth once the temperature rises into the mid-30s Celsius (mid-90s Fahrenheit). In severe cases, high temperatures and direct sunlight can cause patches of bark on newly planted trees to split open.

High winds, especially from a single prevailing direction, can cause considerable structural damage to plants. Although this is often seen as a winter problem, many plants are most at risk when they are fully laden with flowers or fruits, especially just after a period of rain when they have the extra weight of all the trapped water on the flowers and leaves.

Nutrient deficiencies

Another common reason for a plant to fail to thrive is nutrient deficiency – that is, the lack of one or more of the mineral salts that are

Plants that are not hardy can be damaged by changes to the environment; frost and low temperatures are amongst the most common causes of damage to plants in the autumn and spring.

essential for healthy plant growth. The nutrients most essential to plant growth are:

- nitrogen, phosphorus (phosphates) and potassium (potash), which are required in large amounts and are referred to as major nutrients
- boron, calcium, chlorine, copper, iron, magnesium, manganese, molybdenum, sodium, sulphur and zinc, which all required in much smaller amounts and are referred to as minor (or trace) nutrients

All plants require these nutrients but in different amounts, depending on the soil type and condition as well as the type of plant being grown.

To make matters more complicated, these nutrients interact. For example, if too much potassium is given to a plant, such as a tomato, it will lead to a deficiency of magnesium. Adding too much fertilizer to try to cure a problem quickly creates its own problems. If high levels of fertilizer are added to soils where potatoes are growing, the skin of the tubers is damaged, and a hard, toughened, knobbly surface, referred to as 'alligator skin', develops.

The problems created by these imbalances become apparent only when symptoms such as thin, spindly growth, discoloured leaves or stem wilt are noticed. Deficiencies also show as poor fruit set or damaged crops, as with tomatoes, which

A lack of nutrients can lead to discoloration, distorted growth or even death if not treated in time.

suffer from blossom end rot, a symptom of calcium deficiency. The storage quality of apples (*Malus*) and many other fruits may be poor because of a problem such as bitter pit, which is also caused by a lack of calcium. Often deficiencies will only be noticed when the symptoms become extremely acute, even though they may have been affecting the plant for a period of time already.

pests and diseases and the environment

Most of the pests and diseases that attack plants in the garden are present in one form or another most of the time. For example, a small population of a pest may be completely unnoticed, and both pests and diseases spend part of the year in a dormant or resting phase.

Some pathogens can remain in a resting phase for up to 25 years before a suitable host comes along and the pathogen becomes active again.

Environmental effects on diseases

To spread and develop successfully, many pathogens must have the right environmental conditions, but exactly what these are will depend entirely on the problem. The two types of mildew (powdery and downy), for example, are unlikely to be seen together, simply because they thrive in completely different conditions.

Bacterial rots prefer damp air around the foliage and branches, with light wounds to the bark or young shoots and flowers to aid invasion.

Cankers prefer damp air around the foliage and branches, with light wounds to the bark or pruning cuts to aid invasion. Poor drainage can also be a significant factor in the spread of the disease.

Downy mildews prefer damp air around the foliage, little movement of air and dead and rotting plants and plant debris close by. They can spread at any time of year.

Powdery mildews prefer conditions where plants are suffering from water stress (caused by either drought or erratic watering), with light moisture over the leaves. This tends to be a summer or autumn disease, and it is usually young, soft foliage that is most vulnerable.

Leaf spots are more of a problem when growing conditions are poor, when plants are poorly fed, and when a film of moisture covers the leaves.

Root rots rely on a number of factors, including plant stress (particularly for honey fungus) and poor drainage (for forms of *Phytophthora*). Most root rots will enter through some form of injury to the root system.

Rusts prefer conditions where the plants are suffering from water stress (either from drought or erratic watering), with moisture over the leaves. This tends to be a summer or autumn disease.

Viruses need some form of sap transfer, which can be achieved by insects, humans or injury. Ideally, the plants should be actively growing.

Wilts prefer damp air around the foliage and branches, with light wounds to the bark or pruning cuts to aid invasion.

Fungi can lie dormant on a plant for months before being activated by the ideal conditions. Then they develop rapidly, producing countless spores to infect neighbouring plants.

Environmental effects on pests

For many pests, warm temperatures, actively growing plants, few natural enemies and a source of food are the main environmental requirements for success.

Aphids prefer actively growing plants and mild temperatures. They seem to be attracted to plants that are already under stress, such as those suffering from drought.

Beetles will eat both soft and woody material, as both adults and young have strong mouthparts. They prefer mild weather and somewhere to shelter.

Butterflies and moths are not particular problems, but their larvae (caterpillars) eat large quantities of food, which is usually soft and leafy as many (but not all) have weak mouthparts. They prefer mild weather or somewhere to shelter.

Eelworms (nematodes), whether they are soil- or surface-borne types, do best when there is a film of moisture over the surface of the host plant.

The **larvae of flies** need large quantities of food, often soft, such as fruits, because many have weak mouthparts. They prefer mild weather or somewhere to shelter.

Mites prefer actively growing plants and warm, dry conditions.

Scale insects and mealybugs prefer actively growing plants and warm conditions.

Woodlice thrive in warm, moist conditions and are often attracted by decaying plant material.

Slugs and snails thrive in cool, damp conditions and when there is a film of moisture over the surface they will travel over. They are usually more of a problem in damp, shaded conditions.

Thrips prefer actively growing plants, which are under stress from lack of water or erratic watering, and warm conditions.

chemical pesticides:
how they work

It is easy to assume that if a chemical is used to control a pest or disease, it will do its job and that is the end of the matter. However, this may not always be the case, because chemicals differ considerably both in their method of application and in the way they work.

Although a pesticide is, strictly, a chemical used to kill pests, including insects, mites and nematodes, the word is also used more generally to mean fungicides, herbicides and animal repellents, and this broader sense is adopted here.

Most of the pesticides used in the garden work effectively by making contact with the pest they are to control, which is achieved in one of two ways:

- targeting the pest specifically with a direct application (which is not easy if the pest is small)
- covering the surface on which they feed or grow

The chemicals used in these ways are generally known as 'contact' pesticides.

Other chemicals are applied to the plant through the roots or leaves so that they can circulate through the sap system. These are known as 'systemic' pesticides, and they kill insects as they suck the sap or eat into the plant's tissue. Systemic pesticides are usually more persistent than contact ones and can remain active in the plant for several months.

The chemicals that rely on direct contact with a pest or disease often work more effectively as a preventative measure and should be applied when a problem is suspected, rather than when definite symptoms appear. This can be particularly useful for fungal diseases that have appeared at about the same time in previous years – spraying the plant just as the spores are coming into contact will kill them or suppress germination before the disease can become established. Alternatively, the germinating spores are killed as they penetrate into the plant's tissue.

The chemicals used on biting or chewing pests work in different ways. Some attack the central nervous system, while others are stomach poisons and have to be ingested by the insects before they start to be affected. On occasions, the effect can be more subtle, with the pesticide suppressing the pest's appetite so that it starves to death.

Although there is a trend away from inorganic pesticides, some have distinct advantages. Pirimicarb-based treatments are effective for controlling aphids but do no harm to other insects, such as ladybirds, which often feed on aphids.

Remember that chemicals on their own are not an effective method of pest and disease control without other measures, such as good hygiene and providing plants with good growing conditions.

Many gardeners have become used to the idea of spraying plants, and even whole areas of the garden, with chemicals in order to grow stronger healthier plants.

Resistance

Over-use or too frequent use has allowed some pests and diseases to build up a resistance (or tolerance) to some of the chemicals that have been used over a period of time. For this reason, it is advisable to change the chemicals you use fairly often. Always check the name of the active ingredient – this is what must be rotated, not the brandname.

Persistence

The speed at which a chemical pesticide breaks down and loses its effectiveness will depend on a number of factors:
- exposure to sunlight
- soil type (if it is applied to the soil)
- temperature
- the chemical structure of the pesticide

Some chemicals, such as DDT, are so persistent that over a period of years the levels found in the environment have gradually increased. For this reason, they have been withdrawn from use and replaced by less persistent products.

Just about every chemical currently available to the gardener will persist for a maximum of three weeks before all traces have gone. Most of the chemicals used now pose no threat to children, pets or wildlife once they have dried on the leaves. However, no chemical is totally safe, so always read the label before using it.

Powder-based chemicals can be applied to plants to give a more localised control for specific problems in a restricted area of the garden.

Due to safety and environmental regulations being regularly improved and updated, chemicals are constantly being tested and re-evaluated. For this reason, the products available to the gardener are constantly changing. This process will continue as newer, more efficient and less environmentally harmful chemicals are introduced, resulting in the withdrawal of older products, although the choice of pesticides available may reduce.

chemical pesticides:
formulation and application

Pesticides are formulated in different ways to suit a range of different situations and reasons for application. This is done to make application easier and more efficient so that the chemical can act quickly to control the pest or disease.

Formulation is the word that is used to describe the type (or form) of product the chemical has been made into – gas, vapour, liquid or solid.

Aerosols
Specially pressurized liquid forms of pesticide deposit a fine layer of minute droplets over the surface of the plant. They are not as popular as they used to be, because of the harmful effects the propellants have when released into the atmosphere.

Baits
Dusts or powders are mixed with an attractant to form a pellet that will entice the pest to come and eat or, in the case of ants, to collect the bait and take it into the nest to kill the future generations.

Dusts
Pesticides in a solid form are mixed with a harmless carrier to dilute them to the correct concentration of active ingredient. They are applied by means of a puffer pack, which releases a fine dust over the plants or over

certain surfaces (in the case of ant powders). Unfortunately, these tend to leave a visible deposit over the plants.

Fumigants
A fumigant should be applied only in a confined space, such as a greenhouse or conservatory. Usually a combustible material, such as paper or cardboard, is impregnated with the active ingredient, and then the chemical is released into the air as it burns.

Other chemicals may be vaporized from a warm surface, releasing the active ingredient into the air.

Granules
A dust is formulated into pellet form, which releases the active ingredient into the soil over a period as the outer coating of the pellet breaks down.

Granules are particularly useful for soil-borne pests. Working on the same principle, cardboard pins impregnated with chemicals can be placed in pots to release chemicals into the compost.

Liquid drench
A drench is similar to a spray (see below), but the main differences are that they are applied in a more concentrated form (usually to the soil) and are not applied under pressure, as a spray is.

Liquid sprays are still the most common method of applying pesticides in the garden, and protective clothing should be worn whenever necessary.

Rooting powders

The powder contains a synthetic plant hormone that promotes the production of callus and roots on cuttings and also, often, a fungicide to protect the cuttings from fungal rots.

Seed dressings

Dusts are mixed to form a paste that will coat seeds with a fungicide or insecticide to protect seedlings and young plants from specific pests and diseases as they germinate and grow.

Sprays

Liquid sprays are the most widely used method of applying a pesticide, with many now available as ready-to-use pre-diluted products or as a concentrated liquid or wettable powder. This diluted chemical can be applied as a fine mist from a sprayer. The aim is to leave a fine, uniform layer over the whole plant, although this is not quite as important if systemic insecticides are used. Thorough application of any pesticide can help to rectify a problem quickly.

SAFETY:

● Chemicals should always be stored safely and in the right conditions – ideally, a frost-free, well-ventilated store without direct access for sunlight. Fluctuating temperatures and bright sunlight will cause the chemicals to break down, becoming less effective at controlling pests and diseases.

● Always keep pesticides out of the reach of children – if possible, keep them in a secure, locked cupboard – and in their original containers so there is no possibility of confusion.

● For safety's sake, never decant pesticides into plastic drinks bottles or leave them lying around where someone else could find them.

organic pesticides:
how they work

Organic pesticides, which are now widely referred to as bio-pesticides, include those treatments where a parasite or predator is involved in killing or controlling a particular pest or disease.

There is a widely held belief among advocates of organic gardening that organically based controls are safer than those based on inorganic or synthetically produced chemicals. While it is true that there appears to be no threat to the environment from using biological controls, many of the organic compounds can be harmful to a wide range of insects and animals as well as those targeted for control.

Standard 'organic' chemicals, such as derris (rotenone) and pyrethrum, not only kill a wide range of insect pests but are also highly toxic to bees and fish, although they are not persistent and leave little residual deposit within the plant, making it possible to eat produce within a day of spraying. The fungicidal Bordeaux mixture (copper sulphate and lime) is also harmful to bees and fish, mammals should be kept away from treated areas for three weeks, and repeated use can severely reduce the worm population in the soil.

Many of the treatments used are similar in effect and function to inorganic pesticides. They can act:

- as a stomach poison, so that as the pest eats plant tissue coated with chemical it is poisoned as it swallows and digests the food
- as an appetite suppressant – for example, the biological pesticide bacteria *Bacillus thuringiensis* is sprayed on the leaves of brassicas, and as caterpillars feed, they swallow the bacteria, which grow inside them and suppress their appetite so they starve.
- by disrupting breathing, as the insect is coated with pesticide, which blocks its breathing holes and suffocates it.

Some fungicides create a residue on the leaves, which make it an inhospitable place for fungal growths and spores, causing them to shrivel and die. Materials such as sulphur and copper-based fungicides are the mainstay of the organic armoury, although there are drawbacks to their use, because many plants are sensitive to copper-based sprays, which lead to leaf spotting and russeting on the fruits of many apples (*Malus*); the pear cultivar 'Doyenne du Comice' is particularly sensitive.

Live insects, as adults, juveniles or eggs, can be introduced to feed on or infect plant pests with a bacterium, fungus or virus, which will ultimately kill the pest. These treatments have the advantage of being specific and have no adverse environmental impact. A good example are the eelworms (nematodes) introduced to control pests such as slugs: the eelworms enter the slug's

Some pests can be controlled by using natural predators to attack and kill a plant pest. Here a predatory mite is attacking a red spider mite.

body and cause septicaemia to develop. This kills the host, which becomes a breeding site for more eelworms, which disperse into the soil in search of another host.

More obvious physical controls are also used. Sticky glues are used to trap insects and hold them until they die of exhaustion or starvation. This can be targeted not just at a specific pest, but even a specific gender, such as the male codling moth (*Cydia pomonella*). This is a development of the traditional grease band, which is fastened around trees to trap female winter moths (*Operophtera brumata*) and prevent them from climbing into trees to lay eggs.

Many new products are being researched at present to find alternatives to inorganic chemicals. Most are based on natural plant extracts or elements – garlic, neem (*Azadirachta indica*), sulphur and even skimmed milk – which in a concentrated or slightly changed form will kill insects or control fungi or bacteria. Many gardeners believe that these 'natural' plant derivatives are the most likely source of the next generation of pesticides.

Barriers can be used to break the life cycle of a pest. Here a grease band traps insects as they try to climb into a plant to lay their eggs.

organic pesticides:
formulation and application

Organic pesticides range from the fairly standard formulations for inorganic pesticides (see pages 18–19) to live insects and bacterial spores in a dormant state or even, in the case of some predators, active adults or young.

When 'live' material is used, it is important to consider how it will be kept alive until it is applied to control a pest or disease because the storage life is limited. Where the pesticide is a formulation, such as a dust and liquid, it can be stored for longer, but all bio-pesticides must be relatively fresh when they are applied.

Bait
Dusts or powders are mixed with an attractant to form a pellet that will entice the pest to come and eat or, in the case of ants, to collect the bait and take it into the nest to kill the future generations.

Barrier
An obstacle of some kind will prevent, trap or deter insects from passing over it to reach a host plant.

Card
Some insect parasites arrive attached to cards, which are hung on plants close to the feeding site of the pest. When the parasites hatch, they move from the card to the plant and start feeding on the pest. The parasitic wasp *Encarsia formosa*, which is used to control whitefly, is usually introduced to greenhouses in the form of cards bearing the wasp larvae.

Dust
A pesticide in a solid form is mixed with a harmless carrier to dilute it to the correct concentration of active ingredient. It is applied by means of a puffer pack, which releases a fine dust over the plants or over certain surfaces (in the case of ant powders). Unfortunately, it tends to leave a visible deposit over the flowers, leaves and stems of the plants.

Fumigants
A fumigant should be used only in a confined space, such as a greenhouse or conservatory. A combustible material, such as paper or cardboard, is usually impregnated with the active ingredient, and the chemical is released into the air as it burns. Other chemicals may be vaporized from a warm surface, releasing the active ingredient into the air.

Granules
A material that insulates and protects insect adults, eggs and larvae of the bio-pesticide in transit allows it to be sprinkled evenly over the leaves of the affected host plant. The cocoons of the aphid-controlling

A beneficial insect, like this small wasp, will lay its eggs inside the scale stage of whitefly, killing the young whitefly and preventing the next generation developing.

Aphidoletes spp., for example, can be mixed with vermiculite before release to ensure even distribution.

Liquid drench

A drench is similar to a spray and can be a liquid or wettable powder, but the main differences are that the drench is applied in a more concentrated form (usually to the soil or compost) and is not applied under pressure as a spray is. Eelworms (nematodes) are often applied in this form.

Pheromone trap

A tent-like structure with a sticky base and a capsule of pheromone (sexual attractant for insects) is suspended in a tree. The male insects are trapped and killed, to prevent them breeding. The traps can also be used to help indicate the correct timing of a spray by indicating the numbers of the pests that are present in a garden.

Spray

Liquid sprays are the most widely used method of applying pesticides, many of which are available as ready-to-use, pre-diluted products or as concentrated liquids or wettable powders (in the case of bacteria). This diluted material can be applied as a fine mist from a sprayer. The aim is to leave a fine, uniform layer over the whole plant.

Pheromone traps act as a method of control or as a means of monitoring populations.

Sticky traps

Brightly coloured cards (the colours chosen to attract particular insects to them) are coated with a non-drying glue, which traps the insect and holds it until it dies of exhaustion. Yellow cards, for instance, are used to trap whitefly. Non-drying glue can also be used around containers to deter vine weevils, ants and woodlice.

Traps

A range of vessels can be filled with a variety of baits to attract pests such as slugs into a feeding site from which there is no escape. Alternatively, hiding places, such as straw-filled pots, will attract earwigs for easy elimination.

biological control of pests and diseases

Although we like to think of biological control as something modern, it has been in use for at least 1700 years in China, where ants were used to combat pests in citrus trees. Gardeners would even place bamboo canes in the trees so that the ants could move from tree to tree without going down to the ground.

This method of control involves the introduction and management of the natural enemy of a particular pest or disease in order to reduce its population to a level that no longer poses a serious threat to the plant. If managed correctly, the biological control will have little or no environmental impact, and no pollutants are produced that might be harmful to the gardener using them. The agents have been selected to control a specific pest (or range of pests) rather than having the 'blanket' effect that was often the case with early chemical controls.

Although these bio-pesticides are increasing in use and popularity, they still account for only approximately 2 per cent of pest and disease control worldwide. Some of this is probably because the range of biological controls is still quite limited. Bio-pesticides are of three main types: parasites, predators and pathogens.

Parasites

A parasite feeds on its host (the plant pest) to complete its lifecycle. For example, the parasitic wasp *Encarsia formosa* lays its eggs inside the juvenile whitefly, and as the egg hatches, the larva eats its way out, killing the whitefly in the process.

Parasite	Pest controlled
Anagrus atomus	greenhouse leafhopper
Aphidius colemani	aphids
Dacnusa sibirica	leaf miner
Diglyphus isaea	leaf miner
Encarsia formosa	whitefly
Metapohycus helvolus	scale insect
Opius spp.	leaf miner

Predators

A predator preys on its host, feeding on it at one or more stages of its lifecycle. For example, the predatory mite *Phytoseiulus persimilis* eats eggs and adults of greenhouse red spider mite. At the present time there are predatory mites, flies and beetles available, all used for controlling specific plant pests.

Predator	Pest controlled
Amblyseius spp.	thrips
Aphidoletes spp.	aphids
Cryptolaemus montrouzieri	mealybugs
Delphastus spp.	whitefly
Hypoaspis miles	sciarid fly (fungus gnat)
Phytoseiulus persimilis	red spider mite

Sticky traps are very effective but they can catch insects that you didn't intend to trap.

Pathogens

Like any other form of life, pests are susceptible to ailments and diseases, and these can be used by gardeners to help control pest populations.

The bacteria *Bacillus thuringiensis* can be sprayed over the leaves of plants such as cabbages, so that when caterpillars feed on the plants they ingest the bacteria, which will stop them eating and cause them to starve to death.

Other bacteria and viruses can be introduced into a pest by using eelworms (nematodes) as the carrier. Once in contact with the host that they attack, the biological agent is transferred into its body, so although the eelworms are involved, it is the virus or bacteria that actually kills the host. Often, the eelworms will reproduce inside the corpse, producing infected young to find new, healthy hosts.

Pathogen	Pest controlled
Heterorhabditis megidis	vine weevil
Phasmarhabditis hermaphrodita	slugs
Steinernema carpocapsae	cabbage root fly, chafer grub, cutworm, leatherjacket, vine weevil

Change of thinking

Perhaps one of the most difficult aspects of biological control is the notion of not trying to eliminate a particular pest or disease completely, because once the problem has been eradicated, the cure will die from lack of food or failure to complete its lifecycle. Ideally, there should always be a small, constant population of pests to support a small population of its natural enemy, so that control is ongoing, rather than the peaks and troughs that are the norm with a spraying regime.

Sprays can still be used but not usually while the biological control is present. It is important not to spray with persistent pesticides just before introducing a predator or parasite. Stop using derris (rotenone) two weeks before the insects are introduced, although pyrethrums can be used until four days before the insects are used, and insecticidal soaps can be used until the day before the insects are released.

integrated pest and disease management

Integrated Pest Management (IPM) is the term used to describe a balanced, overall approach to pest and disease control rather than a fire-fighting approach to individual attacks as they occur. IPM involves the deployment of a combination of all the measures available to the gardener to control plant pests and diseases, and it requires a planned and co-ordinated approach to the whole garden environment through the use of:

- cultural measures, such as growing resistant cultivars, maintaining good hygiene and using companion planting
- organic measures, including pesticides based on naturally derived products, traps and barriers
- biological controls, through the introduction of predators and parasites
- chemical controls, such as inorganic systemic or contact pesticides, which are used only when necessary

As close as possible to the most commonly attacked plants grow plants and create habitats that attract, feed and provide a refuge for beneficial insects, such as lacewings, ladybirds and rove beetles, which feed on pests.

Use mulches and irrigation to help reduce water stress, because plants suffering from water stress are far more susceptible to attack by certain diseases, such as powdery mildew.

Pruning will allow good air circulation and light penetration, which will help keep the incidence of disease to a lower level. Time the pruning to avoid problems – cherries, plums and other members of the *Prunus* genus should be pruned in summer to avoid silver leaf infection, for example.

Remove and burn dead and diseased material, dead plants and prunings as frequently as possible to reduce levels of pests and disease in the garden.

WEED CONTROL:

Good hygiene in the garden includes weed control, because some native plants act as alternative hosts for a number of pests and diseases:

- black nightshade (*Solanum nigrum*) hosts virus-transmitting eelworms, which can also infest aubergines (eggplants), tomatoes, peppers and potatoes
- chickweed (*Stellaria media*) can harbour red spider mite and whitefly
- groundsel (*Senecio vulgaris*) can host certain rusts, mildews and sap-sucking insects, such as thrips and aphids

By using a pest management programme, it is possible to use sprays and beneficial insects to control a range of pests.

Practise good crop rotation to prevent the build-up of a particular pest or disease.

Where possible, select cultivars with a good pest and disease resistance – the carrot 'Flyaway' shows some resistance to carrot root fly, for example – and select cultivars that are best suited to the growing conditions. If you garden where the rainfall is high, choose apple and pear cultivars with some scab resistance, such as the pear 'Louise Bonne of Jersey'. In drier regions choose cultivars with some mildew resistance, such as the dessert apple 'Meridian'. The pear 'Conference' is most suitable for growing in cooler districts.

Use barriers and traps to control and monitor the insect activity within the garden to ensure that sprays are applied only when absolutely necessary. When you do feel you need to resort to chemicals, use the most appropriate insecticide or fungicide to control pests or diseases and apply it before the attack builds up and causes damage. Use only biological control or organic sprays if edible plants are close to being harvested.

Companion planting

Plant companion plants to try to deter pests and diseases before they become a problem. These plants can work in different ways;
- as host plants, which are attractive to certain pests and diseases and draw them away from crop plants
- as repellent plants, which drive pests and diseases away from certain areas or plants

SPRAYING:

Always follow a sensible spraying policy, which includes following the instructions on the carton carefully and wearing appropriate protective clothing. Spray in the late evening, when bees and other beneficial insects are less active, and treat only the infested parts of the plant and the immediate area beyond.

Crop plant	Companion plant
Apples	Wallflower
Broad beans	Carrot, celery
Cabbage	Beetroot, chard
Lettuce	Carrots, radish
Potatoes	Nasturtiums (*Tropaeolum*), marigolds (*Tagetes*)
Raspberry	Marigolds
Rose	Chives, garlic
Strawberry	Borage, onions
Sunflower	Cucumber, sweetcorn
Tomatoes	Basil, carrot

the ten most common plant pests

By the 'ten most common' groups of plant pest, what we really mean is the ten groups that adapt most successfully to their living conditions. They are usually the pests that do one or more of the following:

- are most frequently encountered in the garden
- attack the widest range of plants
- do the most damage
- are the most difficult to control

They are usually capable of adapting to a wide and varied range of environmental conditions and may be found in the house, conservatory or greenhouse as well as living on plants outdoors for at least part of the year.

One such example is the black bean aphid (*Aphis fabae*), which is easily seen and recognized as a tiny black insect usually found in great concentrations on the tips of young shoots. It is a common pest, which can breed rapidly, producing many generations in quick succession. It has been estimated that, in perfect conditions with no predators present, one female is capable of

giving rise to a population of 2,000,000,000,000,000 aphids over a three-month period. It is just as well that this particular aphid has a large number of predators and often quite high mortality rates with each generation, or we would see infestations of epidemic proportions on an annual basis.

The keys to dealing with the problem are vigilance and timing. The main difficulty with an insect attack is that it can easily go unnoticed in the early stages. By the time the plant begins to show signs of suffering, the infestation can be well established and the pest may be present in quite large numbers. Knowing your plants is an invaluable aid to spotting the problem early, as you will quickly notice signs such as leaf discoloration, bud distortion or wilting (when you know the watering has been adequate).

Outdoors, watch for indicators such as ants running up and down the stems of your plants. Because they regularly make use of the secretions of other insects, you may find

that the ants are simply making the most of the situation rather than causing a problem themselves.

Other pests, such as vine weevil larvae, hide away among the roots of the plants, so their presence goes unnoticed until the plant Is really struggling. Containers are particularly attractive for this pest because they offer easy access to the adult and a slightly drier environment than border soil, since the loamless compost often used in containers is much easier to dig through. It can be quite disconcerting to knock a plant from its pot to see what is wrong and discover that the plant has virtually no root system left.

It is important to identify the pest you are dealing with before you take action. Many insects are harmless, if not positively beneficial, to your plants, and to wipe them out would be wrong. These 'goodies' often prey on the smaller pests, helping to keep their numbers under control. Try to get a close enough look to make certain you are actually dealing with a pest.

Ants

Several species of ant can cause problems in the garden, either directly or indirectly, although they are usually more of a nuisance than a real danger to plants. The three main species are black ants (*Lasius niger*), red ants (*Myrnica spp.*) and yellow meadow ants (*Lasius flavus*). These insects live in nests, forming colonies of varying sizes, which last for several years, usually the duration of the queen ant's life span.

The first indication that ants are present in the garden will often be the sudden wilting of plants, which is caused by ants burrowing under plants as they construct their nests. As they remove soil or compost, a plant's roots dry out, and this can be a particular problem on light, sandy soil.

Ants are often seen on plants heavily infested with aphids, mealybugs or scale insects, because they collect the honeydew secreted by these insects to feed the grubs in their nests. This aphid activity will weaken the plant still further, and, to make matters worse, the ants appear to protect the aphids

from predators, allowing the aphid population to increase in number at a quicker rate than normal.

Another major cause of irritation for gardeners can be mounds of earth in a lawn above the point where nests are being constructed. Although this appears to do little harm to the lawn, the soil can wreak havoc on the moving parts of mowing machinery, causing excessive wear and tear, and if the little mounds are not swept away, they form 'caps' in wet weather, which stops the grass from growing.

The main nests are often sited under the paving of paths and patios, which makes it extremely difficult to gain access in order to kill the ants.

Aphids

There are many species of these sap-sucking insects, and few plants seem to be immune from attack. Aphids vary in colour from green to yellow, pink, black, greyish-white or brown. They are usually 2–5mm (up to ⅕in) long, but this can vary depending on the host plant the aphids are feeding on. Juvenile aphids (nymphs) shed their outer skins several times as they grow larger, and these translucent or whitish skins accumulate on the upper surface of leaves as they are shed, while the insects are usually found feeding on the undersides.

Some aphids feed on specific plants and are closely associated with certain plants as a part of their lifecycle – the pea aphid (*Acyrthosiphon pisum*), for example, feeds and overwinters on peas and their relatives. Others, such as the rose root aphid (*Maculolachnus submacula*), will feed only on specific parts of a plant.

In general, affected plants show reduced growth and varying degrees of distorted or stunted leaves and shoots, particularly the tender shoot tips, which the aphids' mouthparts can penetrate more easily. The upper surface of the leaf may become sticky with honeydew excreted by the aphids, and a black sooty mould will often grow on this sticky deposit. A greater threat to plant health is the possible spread of virus disease on the insects' mouthparts as they move around from one plant to another while feeding.

They are all capable of reproducing at a phenomenal rate, especially if they have an adequate food supply and are left alone by humans and natural predators.

Beetles

Beetles and weevils, which are among the insects most commonly seen in the garden, are characterized by their hard outer casing, which often has a tough, shiny, armour-like appearance. They vary in size – from 1mm to

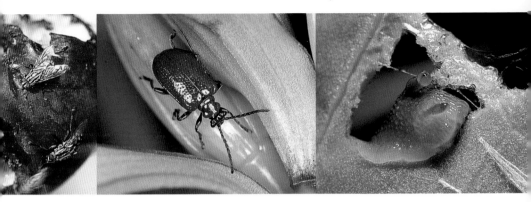

3cm (up to 1¼in) long – and in colour. Although the majority are black, grey or brown, others, such as ladybirds and the lily beetle (*Lioceris lilii*), are brightly coloured.

Beetles will attack a wide range of plants. Some, like the vine weevil (*Otiorhynchus sulcatus*), have numerous hosts, but others, such as the asparagus beetle (*Crioceris asparagi*), feed on only one type of plant. A number of beetles attack and feed on specific parts of plants, and the large number that attack and damage fruit often take their common name from their host plant, including the raspberry beetle (*Byturus tomentosus*) and the apple blossom weevil (*Anthonomus pomorum*). Some prefer vegetables – the turnip gall weevil (*Ceutorhynchus pleurostigma*), for example – while others attack ornamental plants, often with devastating effect, as in the case of the elm bark beetle (*Scolytus* spp.), which feeds on elm (*Ulmus*) trees before laying its eggs and inadvertently spreading the fungus known as Dutch elm disease (*Ophiostoma ulmi*), which is fatal to the trees.

Not all beetles are harmful to plants. Some are beneficial as predators of garden pests – ladybirds feed on aphids (although not all aphids are eaten, as ladybirds find some species poisonous) and ground beetles feed on a number of species, particularly cabbage root fly.

Caterpillars

A caterpillar is the larval stage of a butterfly or moth, which feeds on the leaves, shoots and roots of plants. Most caterpillars have elongated, creased, tubular bodies with a distinctive shiny head. Just behind the head are three pairs of jointed legs on the thorax and between two and five pairs of claspers (prolegs) on the abdomen.

There are many species of butterfly and moth, with over 50 species being regarded as garden pests. The caterpillars range in size from 5mm to 10cm (¼–4in) long, and they also differ widely in colour and the presence of body hair (which acts to deter predators from eating them). Some, such as the tortrix and webber moths, hide under a silken web.

Different species prefer different feeding sites on plants. Most of the pest species feed on leaves, such as the cabbage white butterflies (*Pieris* spp.) and winter moth (*Operophtera brumata*), but others spend part of their life in the soil and feed on plant roots. Some of the these soil-dwelling caterpillars, known as cutworms, spend long periods in the soil. More specialized moths feed almost entirely underground. Some caterpillars, such as the pyracantha leaf miner (*Phyllonorycter leucographella*), live within the leaf, feeding on the inside, or, like the leopard moth (*Zeuzera pyrina*) and goat

moth (*Cossus cossus*), bore into stems. The codling moth (*Cydia pomonella*) eats its way into fruits, and other caterpillars attack berries or seeds. Some have a solitary existence, but the majority live and feed in large groups after the adult female has laid vast numbers of eggs close together.

Eelworms

Correctly called nematodes, these are microscopic, worm-like creatures, often less than 1mm in length. Many play a valuable role in the breaking down of organic matter in the soil, but some are important plant pests. They are capable of causing stunted growth, leaf and stem distortion, dramatic reductions in the production of fruit and flowers and, ultimately, the death of the plants that are attacked. Some will feed within their plant host in the stems, leaves or, in some instances, bulbs. Others live in the soil but feed on or inside the roots of plants they attack. In addition to the damage they cause directly by feeding on host plants, some eelworms are capable of transferring viruses from infected to healthy plants as they suck the sap of their host. A number of the soil-borne eelworms, known as dagger eelworms (*Xiphenema* spp.), are capable of surviving in the soil for many years as eggs, which release juvenile eelworms only when a suitable host is planted close by. These eelworms feed on the roots but do not enter the plants.

Stem and bulb eelworm (*Ditylenchus dipsaci*) and root knot eelworm (*Meloidogyne* spp.) will attack and feed on strawberries, narcissus, onions, phlox and many other plants (over 800 hosts have been recorded), while chrysanthemum eelworm (*Aphelenchoides ritzemabosi*) and potato cyst eelworm (*Globodera rostochiensis* and *G. pallida*) are more frequently associated with specific hosts. All must have moist conditions as they move through the soil or over the leaves and stems of plants on a film of moisture.

Flies

A number of garden pests belong to the fly family, including some leaf miners and midges, as well as flies, although there are also a large number of beneficial insects in this group.

It is the larval stage that is usually responsible for damage to plants. The larvae have a range of preferred plants on which they feed, as well as attacking specific parts of their food host, such as seeds, fruits, roots, stems and leaves. The feeding larvae can do considerable damage as they eat into plant tissue, and this is often made worse as secondary fungal rots affect the damaged areas and continue to develop

even after the larvae have finished feeding and left the plant.

Ornamental plants, vegetables, lawns and all forms of fruit (tree, bush and cane fruit) may be attacked by specific pests. The activity and feeding of some of these pests – the hemerocallis gall midge (*Contarinia quinquenotata*) and yew gall midge (*Taxomyia taxi*), for example – will cause distorted, gall-like growths. Many of the leaf miners lay eggs on the leaves of plants or in the soil close by so that the larvae can invade the leaves of plants shortly after hatching. Others, like the chrysanthemum leaf miner (*Phytomyza syngeniae*), actually insert their eggs, as many as 100 at a time, into the leaves of the host plant. Perhaps the two most commonly seen garden pests in this group are encountered on vegetables: the cabbage root fly (*Delia radicum*) and carrot root fly (*Psila rosae*). Within a few days of hatching, the larvae feeding on the roots of these and closely related plants can devastate whole beds of young plants.

Mealybugs

These soft-bodied, sap-feeding insects are up to 4mm (less than ¼in) long. They are oval and are covered with a white, fluffy wax, which is secreted from the insects' bodies and which also conceals the eggs to protect them. There are several genera, but among those most often seen are *Pseudococcus* and *Planococcus*. Mealybugs will attack a wide range of plants, making them a considerable problem, particularly in greenhouses and conservatories, although they can be found outdoors.

Adults and young can occur on plants at the same time, and in warm, humid conditions they will breed all year round. They frequently infest leaf axils and other inaccessible places on the plant, such as between twining stems or in cracks and crevices in the bark. As the pest feeds, it excretes a sticky honeydew on to the leaves, and this often becomes black after being colonized by sooty mould fungus.

There is a group of mealybugs (*Rhizoecus* spp.) that feed on the roots of plants growing indoors and outside, especially those plants that are growing in fairly dry soil or free-draining compost.

The one mealybug that has a specific host range is the phormium mealybug (*Trionymus diminutus*), which appears to attack only the New Zealand flax (*Phormium tenax*) and the cabbage palm (*Cordyline australis*).

Mites

Mites have eight legs, rather than six, making them relatives of spiders, and although some species are plant pests, many

mites are beneficial to the gardener. They scavenge on decaying plant debris and feed on other mites and insects. Some mites are even used as a biological control of garden pests.

All are less than 1mm long and live in large populations, feeding on a wide range of both indoor and outdoor hosts, including fruit trees and bushes, bulbs and ornamental plants in greenhouses and conservatories, where the mites belonging to the red spider mite group are a particular problem. Fruit tree red spider mite (*Panonychus ulmi*), greenhouse red spider mite (*Tetranychus urticae*) and *Bryobia* mites can cause considerable damage.

They feed by sucking sap from the host plants, causing a fine, pale mottling of the foliage. Heavily infested plants may become festooned with a silken web. Tarsonemid mites attack shoot tips, flowerbuds and young leaves, often causing stunted and distorted growth. As well as sucking sap, gall mites, such as blackcurrant gall mite (*Cecidophyopsis ribis*) and witches' broom gall mites, secrete chemicals as they feed that cause the plant to produce distorted growths, which often enclose the mites.

Most mites prefer warm, dry conditions, and they can reproduce rapidly. Some are capable of transferring viruses from infected to healthy plants as they feed.

Scale insects

These sap-sucking insects attack the undersides of young leaves and the stems of many plants in greenhouses and conservatories, as well as those growing in gardens, particularly where they are growing in sheltered positions.

The adult insect, which remains static, is protected by a white, yellow or brown, shell-like structure (or scale), which it secretes to cover its body. These scales can vary in size according to the species, often reaching to 5mm (about ¼in) across, and may be flat or domed in shape. Brown scale (*Parthenolecanium corni*), soft scale (*Coccuis hesperidum*) and cushion scale (*Pulvinaria floccifera*) are the species most commonly encountered.

Most scale insects lay their eggs under their own bodies, where they are protected by the scale, although the female cushion scales produce white, waxy fibres to protect the eggs. Some females are each capable of producing up to 2,000 young.

Newly hatched scale insects crawl all over the host plant, looking for a suitable feeding site where they will remain for most of their lives. While feeding, some scale insects excrete a sticky, sugary substance, called honeydew, which clings to plant foliage and encourages the growth of sooty mould fungus.

Slugs and snails

There are at least four species of slug that attack garden plants, including the large black slug (*Arion ater*), which grows to 15cm (6in) long, and the garden slug (*Arion hortensis*), which reaches 3–4cm (1¼–1½in) long. A wide range of plants will be attacked and eaten by slugs throughout the growing season and in mild spells in winter, although food is limited at this time of year. Irregular holes are made in the foliage, while the stems and flowers of plants are often eaten away completely. This is especially the case with softer tissue, such as the tender young stems of annuals and herbaceous perennials, although young shoots of woody plants can also be attacked. Slugs will feed above and below ground level, often feeding on plants just before they emerge through the soil. They can vary in colour from black through browns to grey or beige.

Slugs secrete a slimy layer of mucus from their bodies, which helps them move about and may leave a characteristic silvery trail as a clue to their feeding sites. They usually survive the winter as eggs, which hatch into adults in spring in warm, moist conditions.

The snail that most commonly becomes a pest in the garden is the aptly named garden snail (*Helix aspersa*), but others, such as banded snails (*Cepaea hortensis* and *C. nemoralis*), can also damage plants. A wide range of plants are attacked and eaten by snails throughout the growing season. Irregular holes are made in the foliage, stems and flowers of plants, especially those with softer tissue, such as annuals and herbaceous perennials. Snails are most commonly found in alkaline soils, which contain the calcium needed by the snail to form its shell. They are mostly active at night and prefer warm, moist conditions, which makes movement easier for them as they secrete a slimy layer from their bodies as a form of lubrication when moving. Snails can live for several years, hibernating through the winter.

Researchers believe that snails have a strong homing instict and will do their best to get back to the garden or area of land where they originated from. In tests carried out on snails which had their shells marked so that their movements could be traced, it has been discovered that snails will travel for several days to return to their 'home'. So throwing them over the garden fence will not help to get rid of them.

the ten most common plant diseases

Just as with the pests, the ten most common diseases are likely to include the ones that are most adaptable to a range of conditions. On a season-to-season basis, there will be some change in a top ten of specific diseases, because the weather always plays a part. A wet growing season will encourage different diseases from a dry one.

The main problem with many diseases is that their development is slow and difficult to spot until it has taken hold. The spread of honey fungus, for example, begins underground and continues under the outer bark of woody plants, out of sight. The first you may know of its presence is when the plant actually dies. A disease such as this can be difficult to eradicate, but prompt action can at least limit its spread and save other plants in the garden.

Other diseases build up gradually until they become a problem to their host plant but do exhibit visible signs of their presence. A fungal disease such as canker will eventually kill a tree but, in the meantime, will inhibit its ability to flower and fruit. This

means that the problem is worth treating as soon as you notice it. Other diseases may seem minor at first – leaf spots or peach leaf curl, for example, are disfiguring initially – but as they encroach on more of the plant, they will begin to affect its overall health.

Mildew can look like a mild disfiguring of the foliage when it starts, and in some seasons it will remain at this level. If the weather suits the growth pattern of the fungus, however, it can consume the plant and sap all its energy, leaving little for the coming winter or the new season.

Soil-borne diseases are the most difficult to identify, because the way they attack means that the death of the plant is the final stage of the process, yet this is the first sign that you will see. In this instance, it pays to be aware that particular weather and soil conditions will encourage certain diseases and help them flourish. Most soil-borne diseases rely on a plentiful supply of moisture to help them spread, so a wet season will be more hazardous to your plants than a dry one.

Identifying the cause of an attack is crucial to accurate treatment, because you will waste both time and money applying the wrong treatment to the problem. The mottled yellow markings of a virus attack, for instance, can be mistaken for fungal attack or mineral deficiency. Both of these can be treated, but a virus cannot, and by the time you have realized your error, more plants can have been infected, as virus is spread by the action of feeding insects moving from plant to plant around the garden.

A healthy, well-fed plant is always less susceptible to attack than one that has been neglected or over-fed to produce copious, sappy shoots, and good air circulation around the plant will reduce the chance of spores taking hold.

Well grown plants appear to have a much stronger immune system and a better capability to shrug of plant pathogens. This is where good cultivation and cultural techniques such as pruning, feeding and watering are really the basis of a good pest and disease control programme.

Canker

Seen as lesions on the branches and stems of plants and caused by either fungal or bacterial agents, canker causes the death of the reproductive area (cambium) beneath the bark of woody plants. The disease usually spreads in concentric rings, creating a larger and larger, target-like wound, until the branch or stem is girdled and the growth above the diseased area dies after a brief period of wilting, a stage often referred to as dieback. Many of these diseases are referred to as dieback or even sometimes as blight rather than as canker, although it is often a canker lower down on the plant that is the cause. Although the symptoms vary depending on both the specific disease and the host, there are some similarities, depending whether the cause of the canker is bacterial or fungal.

Bacterial cankers can be identified from the dark, sunken lesions on the bark. These are usually wet and often oozing bacterial slime, which is one of the principal methods of spreading the disease. Bacterial canker of

plums and cherries (*Pseudomonas mors-prunorum*) is possibly the most common but is specific to those members of the *Prunus* genus, while another disease, fireblight, which is caused by a bacterium (*Erwinia amylovora*) and is included in wilt diseases, will attack a wide range of hosts, including apples (*Malus*), *Chaenomeles*, cotoneasters, hawthorn (*Crataegus*), pears (*Pyrus*), pyracanthas and *Sorbus*.

Fungal cankers are present when the bark is raised and often roughened around the edges of the open wound, exposing the bare wood beneath, with dry, flaking bark around the wound. Apple canker (*Nectria galligena*) is the most common fungal canker and, despite its name, also attacks ash (*Fraxinus*), beech (*Fagus*), holly (*Ilex*), pears (*Pyrus*), poplar (*Populus*), *Sorbus* and willow (*Salix*).

Downy mildew

This disease is often confused with powdery mildew (see page 40), even though they are not related and actually thrive in different conditions. The symptoms of both types of mildew can, however, be similar.

Downy mildew is seen as areas of yellow or pale green discoloration, which develop on the upper surface of the leaves, with corresponding off-white or faintly purple fungal growth on the underside. As the infection spreads, large areas or even the

entire leaf will discolour and die, sometimes resulting in the collapse of the entire plant.

A wide range of plants can be affected, with downy mildew especially troublesome on specific vegetable plants, including brassica downy mildew (*Peronospora parasitica*), lettuce downy mildew (*Bremia lactucae*) – although this will also attack cinerarias (*Pericallis*), gaillardias and centaureas – and pea downy mildew (*Peronospora viciae*). A number of ornamental plants are also affected by specific forms, such as rose downy mildew (*Peronospora sparsa*) and, in recent years, pansy downy mildew (*Peronospora violae*), which affects winter-flowering pansies, and hebe downy mildew (*Peronospora grisea*), which attacks broad-leaved hebes. Both these latter diseases are capable of killing their host plants in a relatively short time. The increase in their spread has been attributed in part to the milder winters experienced over recent years, because this type of fungus spreads most rapidly in warm, humid conditions and is able to survive dry conditions by producing special resistant spores, which germinate when moisture levels rise.

Honey fungus

Although technically a root or basal rot, honey fungus (the collective name for a

number of *Armillaria* spp.) is important enough to be listed separately. It is possibly the worse fungal disease to invade any garden, because there is so little that can be done to control it and it is almost impossible to eradicate. There are several strains of honey fungus, including:

- *Armillaria mellea*, the most destructive
- *Armillaria gallica*, which usually attacks only plants that are under stress for another reason, such as waterlogging or drought
- *Armillaria ostoyae*, which seems to prefer to attack conifers
- *Armillaria tabescens*, which feeds on dead wood rather than attacking live material

Some of these forms of honey fungus are capable of killing large, mature trees within three to four years of infecting them, although there are cases of the fungus and host plant living together for many years before the plant succumbs and dies.

The initial symptoms often show as premature leaf yellowing and leaf fall in autumn, followed in succeeding years by branches dying back from the tips until the entire top of the plant has died. Flowering plants tend to produce large quantities of seeds, fruits or berries before the plant just collapses and dies or fails to come into leaf in spring.

This fungus can spread through the soil by means of thin, black roots (rhizomorphs), which usually grow about 1m (3ft) a year, or by fungal spores produced in autumn from golden-yellow (honey-coloured) toadstools. The toadstools usually appear around the infected plant only when it has started to die, and each is capable of dispersing 10,000,000,000,000 spores over a five-day period.

Leaf spots

There are a large number of fungi and some bacteria that cause spots to appear on the leaves of plants. These spots are usually circular, but they may have irregular boundaries, and they are most commonly grey or brown in colour, although rhododendron leaf spot (*Gloeosporium rhododendri*) often causes purple or brown spots with purple margins. As individual spots on the leaves develop and increase in size, they may join together, causing large areas of dead leaf tissue to form. When this stage of development is reached, the leaves may be killed, causing the defoliation of badly infected plants, which in turn may retard the overall growth of the plant. This is especially the case with blackspot of roses (*Diplocarpon rosae*).

Bacterial leaf spots are seen as dead patches of cells on the leaves, usually

circular or irregular in shape, but always with a yellow margin (or halo) around them – as, for instance, in halo blight of beans (*Pseudomonas ssyringae* pv. *phaseolicola*) – and an absence of raised fungal fruiting bodies as seen on fungal leaf spots. Some bacterial leaf spots also have moist areas in the centre of the dying area of tissue.

Fungal leaf spots are often seen as a slightly depressed area, where the tissue has died, with a slightly raised margin as the plant's immune system tries to combat the spread of the disease. This is a large group of diseases – there are six different leaf spot diseases affecting members of the cabbage family alone.

Powdery mildews

This is possibly one of the most easily recognizable diseases seen in the garden. It usually shows as a white, powdery, felt-like growth spreading over the upper surface of the host plant's leaves, although there are exceptions, including rhododendron powdery mildew (*Erysiphe* spp.), which produces yellow patches on the upper side of the leaf and a buff-coloured, felt-like growth on the underside; and strawberry mildew (*Sphaerotheca macularis*), which shows as dark reddish blotches on the tops of the leaves and a corresponding grey fungal growth on the underside

Other symptoms include distorted leaves and shoots in rose powdery mildew (*Sphaerotheca pannosa*). American gooseberry mildew (*Sphaerotheca mors-uvae*) not only causes the leaves to become distorted and fall prematurely but also so badly infects the fruit that they split open. With grape powdery mildew (*Uncinula necator*), leaves, flowers and fruits can all be severely damaged. Cucumber powdery mildews (there are at least four) can have the same devastating effects as well as being a source of fungal spores that spread to marrows and courgettes (zucchini). Apple powdery mildew (*Podosphaera leucotricha*) can cause leaf distortion as well as severe damage to the new shoots as they develop in spring and early summer, and this can affect the cropping potential of the trees in later years. This particular strain of fungus is also known to attack medlar (*Mespilus*), pear (*Pyrus*) and quince (*Cydonia*) but not with the same severity.

This disease is always worse on plants that are growing in dry conditions, particularly when the plants are under stress from lack of water.

Moulds

There are only a few moulds, but one particular species, grey mould (*Botrytis cinerea*), has one of widest host ranges of

any fungus that attacks garden plants, growing both outdoors and under protection. This fungus will attack leaves, flowers, stems and fruits of plants, causing tissue to decay and covering the infected areas with a grey, fur-like mould.

Sooty mould (*Cladiosporium* spp.) can also be seen on a wide range of plants but appears to be quite harmless and non-pathogenic to plants.

This disease is more commonly associated with sap-sucking insects that excrete honeydew on to the leaves and fruits of plants. However, accumulated sooty mould will have a detrimental effect on plant growth because it stops sunlight reaching the leaves, and some badly affected plants shed any leaves that are completely covered with sooty mould.

There is also a fungal disease of turf called snow mould (*Monographella nivalis*), which used to be known as fusarium patch. Snow mould causes areas of dead grass to form as the disease spreads across the turf. This shows as yellowish-brown patches with off-white or off-pink margins to the affected areas, and in a severe attack these patches may merge to form areas up to 1m (3ft) across. Often the leaves of the affected grass have a slimy texture as the fungus invades the living tissue.

Root rots

An enormous group of diseases, root rots are characterized by a breakdown of the cells that make up plant tissues, which are reduced to a rotting mass. In general, this type of rot affects the roots or base of the plant, with some being referred to as root rots and others as basal rots, although it is often difficult to distinguish exactly where the infection actually started.

Some of these diseases are fungal rots and others are bacterial. Some diseases seem to affect woody plants, while others only affect herbaceous plants and vegetables.

A disease like phytophthora root death (*Phytophthora* spp.) can affect a wide range of woody plant hosts, and it is one of the most common causes of death among trees and shrubs. It is particularly common on wet, heavy or poorly drained soils. Strains of this disease may remain dormant in the soil for many years before the ideal conditions – usually a combination of soil moisture level and soil temperature – for growth and infection occur.

Many seedling basal rots come into this group, as do some of the most troublesome lawn grass diseases, including red thread (*Laetisaria fuciformis*), fairy ring (*Marasmius oreades*) and dollar spot (*Sclerotinia homoecarpa*), which can devastate fine turf.

Among the diseases that affect herbaceous plants, red thread of strawberry (*Phytophthora fragariae*) causes the whole plant to collapse and gets its name from the resulting red centre to the plants roots, which is caused by the toxins produced by the fungus. A bacterial rot of potato, blackleg (*Erwinia carotovora*), causes both the stems and tubers of potatoes to rot and is carried over from one year to the next on infected potato tubers.

Rusts

A large group of fungal diseases affecting the leaves and stems of plants, often showing as yellow or pale green blotches on the upper surface of the leaf. On the underside clusters of blister-like structures – from blackish-brown, through brown and orange to white (depending on the particular type) – can be found. These burst open releasing spores, which infect other plants.

Plants which can be attacked include many ornamental species, ranging from antirrhinums – antirrhinum rust is *Puccinia antirrhini* – to woody plants, like roses (rose rust is *Phragmidium tuberculatum* and *P. mucronatum*). Some herbaceous perennials, particularly geraniums, hollyhocks (*Alcea*) and iris, can be devastated and even killed after several successive attacks. Many vegetables suffer from rusts, including asparagus, leek and lettuce. Mint (*Mentha*) can be particularly badly infected. Trees, conifers and houseplants suffer several different types of rust.

Some forms of rust have complex lifecycles, spending time on two quite different hosts. Wheat rust spends part of its life living on members of the Berberidaceae family, including mahonia, and plum rust spends time on some species of anemone. Control of these species can be achieved by not growing joint hosts close together, which prevents the lifecycle being completed.

Viruses

Virus is a generic word used for a wide range of diseases affecting a vast number of plants. Often, one type of virus, such as cucumber mosaic virus, will infect almost any plant it comes into contact with. Viruses do not have botanical names like other diseases; instead they are named for their characteristic symptoms, such as leaf roll virus, the plant on which the virus was first identified, or a combination of the two, such as arabis mosaic virus.

Commonly seen symptoms of viral infection include stunted growth (which affects the whole plant) and various degrees of distortion, mottling, ring spotting, dead areas of tissue and mosaic patterning on the leaves or flowers. Flowers may fail

completely or show distortion, or they may form but show colour-breaking, when pale streaks of colour develop on dark petals or vice versa.

Some viruses show only in the fruit, with no leaf or stem symptoms apparent. Chat fruit on apples prevents the fruits developing, star crack fruit and rough fruit affect the skins as they develop. Plum pox virus often shows only as marks, blemishes and sunken areas on plums and damsons.

Infected plants generally crop poorly or not at all. They may die prematurely, although this is rare because the virus needs the host. To make matters more difficult, some viruses may infect certain plants without causing visible symptoms, by the process known as latent infection.

Wilts

These common and widespread diseases can be caused by different agents – bacterial, fungal or viral – but the one thing they have in common is their effect on the plant: they cause the leaves, stems and shoot tips to wilt and collapse. Although the wilting may appear temporary and some plants seem to recover, collapse of the plant is usually the final stage of the disease.

Bacterial wilts include fireblight (*Erwinia amylovora*), which causes wilting of shoot tips and gradual death of the plant.

Characteristic red-brown staining under the bark confirms the presence of this disease in the plant.

Fungal wilts are usually caused by soil-borne spores or fungal particles that invade root or stem tissue. As the fungus develops, it causes a blockage in the tissues carrying liquids around the plant, and this, in turn, causes the plant to wilt. Verticillium wilt (*Verticillium albo-atrum* and *V. dahliae*) will attack a wide range of garden plants, including ornamental trees and shrubs, herbaceous perennials, fruit, vegetables and bedding plants.

Fusarium wilt (*Fusarium oxysporum*) will attack a much wider range of plants and is much more aggressive than the verticillium wilts. Perhaps the best known wilting disease of modern times is Dutch elm disease (*Ophiostoma ulmi*), which causes yellowing of the leaves and death of, first, the shoots and ultimately the whole plant, with large, mature trees being killed within three or four years of the initial infection. All fungal wilts will show different degrees of staining through the stems when they are cut; this is usually as a result of toxins which are produced by the activity of the fungus.

Viral wilts include rose wilt virus, which causes the collapse and death of young roses that have been propagated by budding or grafting.

the ten most common plant disorders

Not all plant problems are as straightforward as a pest or disease. Some develop as a result of a change in circumstances, such as: an accident; localized climatic change, particularly temperature; or the availability of water. Plants need certain conditions to grow well. There is a range in which they will thrive and another in which they will survive. Sudden changes in conditions will interrupt growth, most obviously in late spring, when a sudden frost can kill growing tips, shoots or even whole plants. If the shoot tip is affected, it will cause a change in growth, as other buds compete as replacements. Single stem plants become multi-stemmed and look, as a result, completely different.

Water is crucial to plants: all their functions depend on it. Plants do not eat food; instead, they absorb nutrients in solution through the roots and transport them within the plant using moisture. The cells of a plant are filled with a water-based solution, and non-woody plants depend on these cells being full to maintain their shape. If water is in short supply, the amount within the cells is reduced, causing them to shrink, which we see as wilting. If the water supply remains interrupted, the cells lose contact with each other, known as the 'permanent wilting point'. Beyond this point it is virtually impossible to rescue the plant, even if the water supply is restored.

The instinctive reaction to seeing a wilting plant is to soak it, but this can do more harm than good. Roots also need air to function, and if they are sitting in water, with no available air, the plant effectively drowns. Aquatic, marginal and bog plants have evolved to grow in water or permanently wet soil, so if part of your garden is wet, plant tolerant species there rather than ones that need good drainage.

Many common disorders faced by plants in the gardens can be eliminated by: regularly feeding and watering; keeping the plants healthy; careful use of chemicals; and planting appropriate varieties.

Other disorders are simply quirks of nature and have to be accepted as part of the fun of gardening.

Bolting

Bolting is the premature flowering (and/or seed production) of vegetable plants, particularly beetroot, celery, lettuce, onion, spinach and cauliflowers. The cause varies from crop to crop and even from cultivar to cultivar of the same species. Common causes, however, are exposure to cold or drought at a critical stage of growth for certain periods.

There is no real way to prevent bolting that is caused by temperatures of 4–6°C (39–43°F) apart from selecting and growing cultivars that have been bred for resistance. Early cultivars of vegetables are more likely to bolt, simply because they are more likely to experience the cold temperatures that cause the condition.

Summer-grown vegetables and salad crops are more likely to bolt if they are kept dry during critical stages of growth when the plants are young. This is usually when they have started to develop a number of mature, rather than seed, leaves. If plants are watered erratically or if they suffer a check when they are being transplanted, the resulting delay in development causes the growth pattern to change and flowering may commence.

Chemical damage

Both pesticides and herbicides can cause inadvertent harm to plants. Garden pesticides are intended for application on growing plants, but they can cause damage if they are used:

- at the wrong rate (too high a concentration or too frequently)
- on plants for which they were never intended
- under the wrong climatic conditions, when plants are under stress

The symptoms of damage can range from slight leaf discoloration or scorch through to outright death of the whole plant.

Herbicides (weedkillers) are formulated to kill plants (weeds), but can also harm the plants we wish to grow if they accidentally come into contact with them or are misused in some way.

Hormone weedkillers are particularly damaging, as they are absorbed into the plant and totally disrupt normal growth. Leaves become misshapen and contorted, becoming thickened and twisted with a mottled appearance. Stems are twisted and stunted, often with a pale tip. Fruits and flowers are distorted and fail to develop.

Other chemicals that can scorch or kill plants include:

• paint, which is common with newly painted greenhouses or fences

• creosote and other wood preservatives on wooden structures and fences

• oil and petrol damage to lawns, caused by spillages from mowers and other petrol-powered equipment

• fertilizers and manures used fresh, to excess or too close to plants

• salt on paths in winter, which will lead to the injury or death of nearby plants

Drought

Water is essential for plant growth, as a chemical and as the solvent within which nutrients are dissolved. Plants take up their food in solution, so water shortage in the soil results in damage or death. Plants with large, smooth leaves, like many vegetables, are most vulnerable.

Physiological drought occurs when there is water available but plants are not able to use it, which can happen in winter when the ground is frozen. Conifers and broad-leaved evergreens lose water from their leaves in windy weather but cannot replace it fast enough to prevent foliage scorch. Although wilting leaves are obvious, there are signs to look for before this stage is reached, such as a lack of glossiness of the leaves, followed by a bluish sheen (particularly on lawns). As the water shortage continues, the leaves gradually turn crisp and brown.

Young plants may bolt, producing flowers and seeds prematurely; older plants may abort flowers and fruits before they have fully developed. Provided they are not left too long, wilting plants can recover if watered sparingly, rather than soaking them until they become waterlogged. Overhead sprays to raise humidity also help, but left for too long, the plants will die.

Frost

Some leaves, shoots, flowers and fruits will blacken, wilt and shrivel if they are exposed to a temperature below freezing for as little as 15-20 minutes. The most vulnerable parts are delicate areas, such as flowers, embryo fruits and rapidly growing shoot tips. Some tender plants grown in the house, conservatory or greenhouse will be damaged in temperatures below 10°C (50°F), which can even occur on an indoor windowsill.

Frost damage occurs largely through the formation of ice crystals in the plant's cells, but most of the damage occurs if the temperature drops below freezing quickly or rises quickly while the plant cells still have ice crystals in them. This rapid change of temperature causes the cell walls to rupture, leading to structural damage. The plant tissue starts to collapse and turn black.

Low-temperature damage on more tender plants is seen as a slightly bluish sheen of plants, and the leaves will often hang limply as the internal functions within the plant are disrupted by the low temperature.

Nutrient deficiency

Plants need a balanced diet of nutrients in order to thrive. Some 'major' chemicals, such as nitrogen, phosphate and potassium, are needed in relatively large quantities. Other 'minor' nutrients, such as calcium, zinc, boron and iron, are required in much smaller amounts. All these nutrients are taken up in different quantities, but are needed for balanced growth, and if any one is in short supply, signs of deficiency appear.

The symptoms of each deficiency vary from plant to plant and will depend on the particular nutrient that is deficient. In addition, if more than one deficiency has occurred at the same time, the symptoms may be different again. If major nutrients are deficient, plants will show obvious signs of poor or stunted growth. When a minor nutrient is deficient, the clues may be less obvious. Many plants prefer an acid soil, so if there is too much free lime in the soil, their leaves will change from glossy dark green to yellow before the plant dies. This condition is referred to as lime-induced chlorosis, but the plant is actually suffering from iron deficiency, because the lime prevents the plant's uptake of iron.

Pollution

The most common atmospheric pollutants are carbon monoxide, sulphur dioxide, nitrogen oxides, chlorides, fluorides, ethylene and ammonia. Effects vary from severe, when plants are injured but not killed, through to terminal, when plants are killed outright in a short space of time.

The symptoms vary widely, but the most common are:
- brown or pale blotches or streaks on the upper surface of the leaves and between the veins
- severe scorching or dead areas along the leaf margins

Affected leaves may die and hang on the plant or may fall prematurely. Young plants are more susceptible to damage than older ones, and conifers and broad-leaved

evergreens are more at risk than deciduous plants, which shed their foliage annually anyway. Whether the pollutants are harmless or damaging will depend largely on the amounts present. For example, small amounts of sulphur in the atmosphere are actually beneficial, because they have a fungicidal action on some diseases, such as rose blackspot. Asparagus and some members of the beet family benefit from the presence of some salt in the soil.

Sun damage

Heat, particularly the heat caused by direct sunlight, can be harmful to many plants, and it will affect different parts of the plants, including leaves, flowers, fruit and stems. Sun scorch occurs when hot sun strikes the bark of thin-barked trees, such as beech (*Fagus* spp.), cherry (*Prunus*), maple (*Acer*) or poplar (*Populus*), although any newly planted tree that has been growing close to others is susceptible once it has been transplanted and its trunk is in bright sunlight. Exposure causes patches or strips of bark to die, which results in death on the sunniest side of the trunk, and this leads to reduced vigour and dieback of branches on the affected side of the tree.

Sun scald occurs when developing fruits are exposed to excessively hot sun. Exposed fruits can display a range of damage:

- tomatoes fail to ripen evenly, developing areas of hard green skin around the area where the fruit is attached to the plant; this is called greenback
- other fruits show papery, pale brownish patches on the affected parts almost like sunburn; apples (*Malus*), pears (*Pyrus*), gooseberries and tomatoes are most commonly affected

Waterlogging

Death and damage to plants caused by waterlogging is not all that common in gardens, but it is probably the main cause of ill-health and death for plants growing in containers or pots on the patio or in the house or conservatory. Overwatering causes a lack of oxygen, which damages and eventually kills the plants, as the water drives the oxygen out of the soil or compost.

The earliest symptom is usually the leaves changing gradually from a healthy green to paler green and eventually yellow. At the same time, the plants develop dry, irregularly shaped blotches.

With regular (but not constant) waterlogging, growth and development of the plant gradually stops as its general health begins to decline. For prolonged waterlogging of longer than 10–15 days roots begin to show signs of cellular damage

(often seen as patches of brown or discoloured tissue), and root death starts to set in. The root zone will develop the characteristic stale smell of decay. As a secondary effect of this root rotting, invasion by fungi and bacteria will make the plants even more vulnerable.

Windchill

This problem is commonly associated with conifers, particularly Lawson cypress (*Chamaecyparis lawsoniana*) and forms of cypress (*Cupressus*), and broad-leaved evergreens, such as aucuba, laurel (*Laurus nobilis*) and pyracantha. The growth on one side of the plant will gradually become a duller colour, start to wrinkle and become progressively drier before turning brown, often dying back into the woody stems. The damage is caused by the death of the leaves on the windward side of the plants because of the direct drying effect of the wind, which draws moisture out of the plant's leaves at a far greater rate than it can be replaced. The problem is worse on exposed sites and where the soil is waterlogged or frozen, so that the roots are unable to function efficiently, restricting or preventing the uptake of moisture to replace the water that is being lost from the desiccating effects of the wind. Windchill may also damage deciduous plants, as the overwintering buds

may become desiccated and die. The plants will gradually become lopsided, producing little or no new growth on the windward side.

Windrock

This is a common problem with taller plants, such as young trees, roses, shrubs and climbing plants, which have been recently transplanted and have a large amount of topgrowth in relation to their root system. The leverage that is exerted as the wind blows against the topgrowth causes the plants to rock back and forth, gradually loosening the roots, but it is usually of insufficient force to uproot the plant completely. The rocking has the effect of breaking tender new roots as they grow. It also causes rubbing at the base of the stem, restricting the movement of water and nutrients and allowing fungal or bacterial infections to enter through the open wound.

The constant rocking causes a saucer-shaped depression to form in the soil around the base of the plant. If rainwater fills this depression and the water freezes, the damage to the stem is made worse and the tree may die. This problem is much worse on exposed, windy sites and especially on heavy or poorly drained soils, where plants may be slow to become established and the soil will quickly compact around the base of the plant.

identifying problems

Plants are vulnerable to attack by a wide range of pests, diseases and disorders, but most plant problems tend to target a specific area of the plant, even though these effects may ultimately show up over the entire plant.

1 Rotten buds
Often a pest or disease has been present at an earlier stage of a flower's development, killing the inner tissue before any symptoms are visible.

7 Rotten fruit
An infection or earlier injury may only become evident as fruits ripen and become softer, making spread of the disease more rapid.

2 Insect attack
Sap sucking insects will often feed close to the shoot tips of plants.

8 Eaten leaves
Pests with strong mouthparts can defoliate entire plants when high populations are present.

3 Mildew
Mildews live in the leaves and young shoots but often affect the entire plant.

9 Rusts and spots
This type of problem usually has an effect on the whole plant.

4 Fungus
Some soil-borne fungi that attack plants live in the layer of tissue between the wood and the outer layer of bark.

10 Canker
These open wounds cause water loss as well as being potential sites for further infection or pest attack.

5 Eaten flowers
Some insects have weak mouth parts and can only feed on the softest plant tissue they can find.

11 Eaten roots
Some pests spend at least a part of their life in the soil and often feed on plant roots.

6 Discoloured leaves
Discolouration is a clue to some problem occurring in another part of the plant, such as the roots.

12 Wilted leaves
Wilted leaves can either happen as a result of direct attack or be an indication that something is wrong elsewhere in the plant.

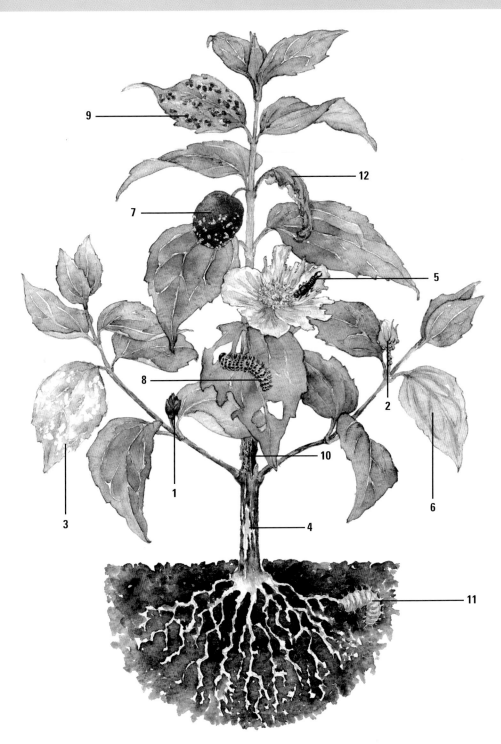

PLANT PROBLEMS:
leaves

The problems that attack leaves can have many causes, but they have one thing in common: they spoil the appearance of the plant you are trying to grow. In some instances, such as leaf miners, this may be an aesthetic problem rather than something that will prove fatal to the plant, and you may decide that instead of using chemicals, you can live with it. In other cases, the damage to the leaves may be an early indication of a potentially dangerous problem that needs your immediate attention before it claims the whole plant.

If the problem is being caused by a creature of some kind, your first task is to identify it. This will give you a clue as to the lifecycle of the pest and when you need to be most vigilant for activity. The speed with which you need to act also depends on the pest, because some, like the caterpillars of the cabbage white butterfly, can cause a huge amount of damage very quickly.

If you use chemicals it is usually important to apply more than one treatment to make absolutely certain that you have dealt with not only the original attack, but also subsequent generations, which may have been eggs during the initial treatment. There are two means of chemical control:

- contact insecticides kill the pests they actually come into contact with, so they must be applied thoroughly to the top of the leaf, the underside and any nearby stems.

- systemic insecticides are taken up inside the plant and carried in the sap, so they affect any pests that feed on the sap; this makes more effective use of the chemical you are applying and means that every feeding pest will be killed as long as the formulation remains active inside the plant, even ones that protect themselves externally, such as scale insects

Always check that the chemical you use is appropriate for the host plant.

Although insects, such as aphids, attack a wide range of host plants, others are more specific to certain hosts. Solomon's seal sawfly attacks only members of one plant genus, *Polygonatum*. So if one of these plants is attacked, you know exactly which others will also need treating.

Many fungal attacks, rots and scabs depend on certain weather conditions. Knowing the disease and the conditions it prefers will mean that you can be aware of the likelihood that it might occur and can be ready to deal with it quickly, before it can cause too much damage. Like pests, many diseases are also quite host-specific, so if you are growing roses, for instance, you will be dealing with problems such as rose rust and can keep a watchful eye on the plant for any signs of attack.

Dealing with an attack accurately and quickly can mean the difference between life and death for the plant.

sap-sucking pests

BLACKCURRANT GALL MITE

Also known as big bud mite, this insect (*Cecidophyopsis ribis*) is an important pest of blackcurrants, and it can spread reversion virus, which dramatically reduces a plant's fruit-bearing.

Symptoms: Buds become swollen and fail to open normally in spring. Distorted leaves form as the sap-sucking mites are released on to surrounding plants.

Plants attacked: Blackcurrants (*Ribes nigrum*), although there are related species of the mite that attack hazel (*Corylus*) and yew (*Taxus*).

Prevention: Remove and burn badly affected plants. As the flowers open, spray with a fungicide based on carbendazim to discourage the mite.

Control: As the buds open, spray with an organic spray, such as those based on fatty acids or rape seed oil.

GREENHOUSE RED SPIDER MITE

These minute mites (two-spotted spider mites; *Tetranychus urticae*) suck the sap of plants and are a serious problem when their populations reach epidemic proportions.

Symptoms: Growth is yellow and stunted. Curled and mottled leaves are covered with a fine webbing made by the insects to cover their breeding colonies.

Plants attacked: Many plants will be attacked, but vines (*Vitis*), carnations (*Dianthus*), chrysanthemums, melons and cucumbers are particularly vulnerable.

Prevention: Spray the undersides of leaves frequently with water and maintain high humidity.

Control: Spray with an insecticide based on a plant extract, such as oil seed rape, at regular intervals as soon as the pest is noticed. Introduce the predatory mite *Phytoseiulus persimilis* to control the pest biologically.

MEALY CABBAGE APHID

This insect (*Brevicoryne brassicae*) will colonize plants and cause stunted, weakened growth, as well as infecting them with a form of mosaic virus.

Symptoms: Yellow patches appear on the upper leaf surface. Dense colonies of grey-green insects covered with a greyish-white, powdery wax coating are seen, usually on the undersides of the leaves but also on the stems of calabrese.

Plants attacked: All members of the Brassicaceae family, particularly the leafy vegetables.

Prevention: Remove and destroy old brassica plants as soon as they have finished cropping.

Control: Spray repeatedly with an organic spray, such as those based on fatty acids or rape seed oil, before introducing lacewing and ladybird (*Cryptolaemus montrouzieri*) larvae as a biological control.

SOFT SCALE

These insects (*Coccus hesperidum*) appear as small, yellowish-brown blisters, 3–4mm (less than ¼in) long, on the undersides of the leaves. They suck the sap, which gradually weakens the plants.

Symptoms: Stunted and distorted growth and a gradual yellowing of the leaves. Plants become weak and susceptible to other pests and diseases. A sticky coating (honeydew) forms on lower leaves, often accompanied by a black sooty mould on these leaves.

Plants attacked: Bay (*Laurus nobilis*), *Citrus* spp., ivy (*Hedera*), *Ficus* spp. and many conservatory and greenhouse plants.

Prevention: There is no effective prevention.

Control: Introduce the parasitic wasp *Metaphycus helvolus*, the predator of scale insect, in midsummer. Apply sprays based on fatty acids in late spring and early summer, when the new scale insects (nymphs) are mobile.

TARSONEMID MITE

The microscopic insects (*Polyphagotarsonemus latus* and *Phytonemus pallidus*) are cream to light brown in colour and are capable of breeding all year round.

Symptoms: Stunted and distorted growth is caused by sap being sucked from young leaves, shoot tips and flowerbuds. Brown, scar-like tissue may form on the stems of badly affected plants.

Plants attacked: Mainly plants growing in greenhouses, houses and conservatories.

Prevention: Remove and burn infested plants.

Control: Spray repeatedly with an organic spray, such as those based on fatty acids or rape seed oil.

THRIPS

Small, aphid-like insects, up to 2mm (less than ⅟₁₆in) long, with fringed wings, varying in colour from yellow to brown. The wingless nymphs are paler. Both adults and larvae feed on the plants.

Symptoms: Fine, light fleck marks are seen on the leaves and also on the flowers and stems. Leaves take on a silvery sheen.

Plants attacked: Mainly plants growing in greenhouses, houses and conservatories, but outdoor plants may also be attacked.

Prevention: Carefully inspect any new houseplants or cut flowers.

Control: Spray with bifenthrin two or three times at two-week intervals. Introduce the predatory mites *Amblysius* spp. as a biological control when the temperature reaches 10°C (50°F).

WHITEFLY

White, winged insects (greenhouse whitefly; *Trialeurodes vaporariorum*) about 2mm (less than ⅟₁₆in) long, that live on the undersides of the leaves. Their excretions leave a sticky deposit (honeydew) on the upper surfaces of the leaves. These sap-sucking insects are able to breed all year round.

Symptoms: Adults fly up from plants in clouds when disturbed. An infestation may cause a mottled pattern on the upper surface of the leaves and a general decline in the plant's health.

Plants attacked: A wide range of greenhouse and houseplants; outdoor plants can also be infested in summer.

Prevention: Not practicable, but introducing the parasitic wasp *Encarsia formosa* into the greenhouse will control the population.

Control: Spray with an insecticide based on a plant extract, such as oil seed rape, at regular intervals as soon as the pest is spotted (this will do minimum harm to the parasite).

DID YOU KNOW?

That it is possible to study the life cycle of some pests and use what you learn to create methods to control them. For example, cabbage and carrot root flies fly below a height of 75cm (2ft 6in) and lay their eggs around the base of young plants, while the cabbage white butterfly is unable to pass through a barrier which has a mesh less than 1cm (½in) wide. This means it is possible to create barriers that will prevent specific pests from reaching their preferred host plants.

biting and chewing pests

CABBAGE WHITE BUTTERFLY

The larvae of the large cabbage white butterfly (*Pieris brassicae*) can cause severe damage on host plants, often completely defoliating them in a matter of days, eating into stems and fouling the rest of the plant with excreta. The larvae of the small cabbage white (*P. rapae*) do similar damage.

Symptoms: Medium-sized, 4cm (1½in) long, yellow and black caterpillars with hairy bodies feed on the leaves and can totally strip away the foliage. leaving only bare stems.

Plants attacked: All brassicas and nasturtiums (*Tropaeolum*).

Prevention: Carefully monitor plants from spring until early autumn.

Control: As soon as the caterpillars are seen, spray with bifenthrin. Introduce the bacterial disease *Bacillus thuringiensis* as a biological control. If the plants are close to harvest use an organic spray, such as those based on fatty acids or rape seed oil.

CHRYSANTHEMUM LEAF MINER

The small insect larvae of the leaf miner fly (*Phytomyza syngeniae*; syn. *Chrymatomyia sygenesiae*) feed inside the leaves of plants.

Symptoms: The leaves have small, pale green or white lines in them, which are the feeding tunnels of the insects. These tunnels are of nuisance value rather than causing serious damage to the plant.

Plants attacked: Chrysanthemums; cinerarias (*Pericallis*), gerberas and pyrethrums (*Tanacetum*) are among the

many relatives of the chrysanthemum also attacked by this pest.

Prevention: Pull off affected leaves as soon as they are seen.

Control: As soon as the insects are seen, spray with imidacloprid at regular intervals.

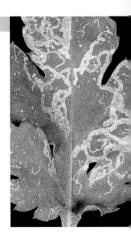

FLEA BEETLE

The brassica flea beetle (*Phyllotreta cruciferae*) can attack and kill seedlings and retard the growth of young plants.

Symptoms: Small beetles, about 3mm (⅛in) long, and blackish-green in colour with a shiny wing casing, eat holes up to 3mm (⅛in) across in the leaves of seedlings and young plants. In addition, the larvae feed on the roots.

Plants attacked: Alyssum, aubrieta, nasturtium (*Tropaeolum*), stocks (*Matthiola*) and wallflowers (*Erysimum*); radishes, swedes and turnips.

Prevention: Clear away plant debris to reduce overwintering sites for adults. Cover seedlings with fleece for the first two weeks after germination.

Control: Spray seedlings with derris (rotenone) or bifenthrin as the seed leaves emerge.

GOOSEBERRY SAWFLY

The larvae of the common gooseberry sawfly (*Nematus ribesii*) can cause severe damage on host plants, often completely defoliating the bushes in a matter of days and gradually weakening the plant.

Symptoms: Small green caterpillars marked with black spots feed on the leaves and totally strip away the foliage, leaving only bare stems and fruits.

Plants attacked: Gooseberries, redcurrants and white currants.

Prevention: Carefully monitor plants from flowering onwards.

Control: As soon as the caterpillars are seen, spray with bifenthrin. If the fruit are ready for picking, use an organic spray, such as those based on fatty acids or rape seed oil.

SLUGWORM

Small adult sawflies (*Caliroa cerasi*) lay their eggs in slits made in the leaves. This insect can have up to three generations each year.

Symptoms: Pale yellow larvae, about 12mm (½in) long, are covered with a black, slimy coating. They feed on the foliage by scraping away the leaf surface, leaving dried brown patches on the leaves.

Plants attacked: Cherries and plums (*Prunus*), hawthorn (*Crataegus*), pears (*Pyrus*), quince (*Cydonia*) and *Sorbus*.

Prevention: Cultivate the soil around the base of the trees.

Control: As soon as the caterpillars are seen, spray with bifenthrin or an organic spray, such as those based on fatty acids or rape seed oil.

SMALL ERMINE MOTH

This pest (*Yponomeuta* spp.) is a small white moth with black markings on the wings. Heavy infestations can totally devastate the foliage of the host plant.

Symptoms: Small caterpillars, 2cm (¾in) long, greyish-green with dark spots, feed in colonies on the leaves. They can totally strip away the foliage, leaving only bare stems. The colonies are covered in a protective web of silken thread.

Plants attacked: Apple (*Malus*), hawthorn (*Crataegus*), cherry (*Prunus*), willow (*Salix*) and many others.

Prevention: Remove and burn any of the shoots that have the web-covered colonies on them.

Control: As soon as the caterpillars are seen, spray with bifenthrin, or introduce the bacterial disease *Bacillus thuringiensis* as a biological control. For fruiting plants that are close to harvest use an organic spray based on fatty acids or rape seed oil.

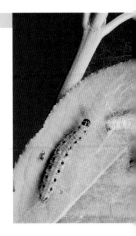

SOLOMON'S SEAL SAWFLY

The adult sawfly (*Phymatocera aterrima*) lays eggs in the stem of the plant as it starts to flower, and the larvae strip the plant's foliage. Although unsightly, plants often recover and will flower the following year.

Symptoms: Greyish-white caterpillars, about 2cm (¾in) long and with black heads, feed on the leaves and completely strip away the foliage, leaving only bare stems.

Plants attacked: Any type of Solomon's seal (*Polygonatum*).

Prevention: Spray the soil around the plants with insecticide just as they come into flower.

Control: As soon as the caterpillars are seen, spray with bifenthrin or an organic spray, such as those based on fatty acids or rape seed oil.

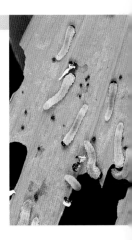

WATERLILY BEETLE

This small beetle (*Galerucella nymphaeae*), yellowish-brown in colour, lays eggs on waterlily leaves in early summer.

Symptoms: Holes and tunnels are eaten in the leaves (pads) of waterlily, with the leaves gradually turning yellow and disintegrating.

Plants attacked: Waterlilies (*Nymphaea* spp.) only.

Prevention: Weighting down the leaf for 24 hours will force the adults and larvae into the water, where they will often be eaten by fish or other insects.

Control: Spray with an insecticide based on a plant extract, such as rape seed oil, at regular intervals (check the carton to ensure it is not harmful to fish).

mildews and scabs

APPLE POWDERY MILDEW

This fungus (*Podosphaera leucotricha*) overwinters in dormant buds and emerges with the leaves to re-infect the plant the following spring.

Symptoms: Leaves are covered with a dense, white, felty mould, with young leaves becoming twisted and distorted, often failing to reach their full size. New shoots may also be infected as they develop, leaving lesions on the branches.

Plants attacked: Cropping and ornamental apples (*Malus*); also medlar (*Mespilus*), pear (*Pyrus*) and quince (*Cydonia*).

Prevention: Grow more resistant apple cultivars, such as 'Discovery' or 'Greensleeves'. Prune out badly infected shoots and thin out branches to allow good air circulation.

Control: As the leaves emerge, start spraying with myclobutanil or a sulphur-based product, according to the manufacturer's instructions.

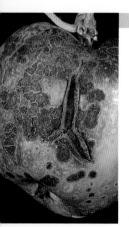

APPLE SCAB

This fungus (*Venturia inaequalis*) survives each year on fallen leaves and infected twigs, and the spores germinate the following spring in warm, humid conditions.

Symptoms: Greyish-green spots on the leaves cause distortion and premature leaf fall. Blister-like lesions appear on the young stems, and black lesions, which become cracked and corky, are seen on the fruits.

Plants attacked: Cropping and ornamental apples (*Malus*), particularly in wet years.

Prevention: Prune to allow good air flow through the tree. Grow resistant cultivars, such as 'Discovery', 'Gavin' or 'Sunset'.

Control: Apply a tar oil wash in winter. Spray with mancozeb from when the buds open onwards.

BRASSICA DOWNY MILDEW

This soil-borne fungus (*Peronospora parasitica*) can invade through the roots and stems and will attack plants at any stage, even the heads of cauliflowers as they develop.

Symptoms: Patches of greyish-white fungal mould are seen on the underside of the leaf with a corresponding yellow blotching on the upper leaf surface. On seedlings and young plants leaves gradually wither and die.

Plants attacked: Any member of the Brassicaceae family, including related weeds and ornamental plants, such as wallflowers (*Erysimum*) and alyssum.

Prevention: Regular weeding. Set individual plants further apart to improve air circulation. Use sterilized pots, trays and compost for propagating young plants.

Control: Apply a fungicide, such as mancozeb, as soon as the symptoms are seen.

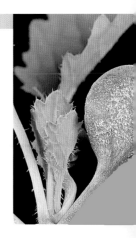

PEACH LEAF CURL

This fungus (*Taphrina deformans*) spreads in cool, damp conditions, especially in a wet spring. The affected plant may become totally defoliated but the second flush of leaves is rarely infected.

Symptoms: Leaves become puckered, blistered and distorted, often changing from green to creamy-white or reddish purple. This is followed by a mould-like growth over the leaf surface before the leaf falls prematurely.

Plants attacked: Peaches, nectarines and related ornamental *Prunus* spp.

Prevention: Prune to allow good air flow through the tree. Clear away and burn all infected leaves.

Control: Spray with a copper-based fungicide in autumn before leaf fall and with mancozeb from when the buds open onwards.

ROSE POWDERY MILDEW

This disease is caused by a fungus, *Sphaerotheca pannosa*, which penetrates the young rose leaves and spreads to the stems and flowers, greatly weakening the plant and sometimes eventually killing it.

Symptoms: A powdery white, felt-like covering forms over the leaves. On young growth the leaf will become distorted, blistered and twisted, often turning yellow and dying prematurely.

Plants affected: This disease is specific to all kinds of roses.

Prevention: Keep plants well watered because powdery mildew is always worse in dry conditions. Prune plants to allow good air circulation. Pick off any infected leaves when first seen. Grow resistant cultivars if available.

Control: Spray with a suitable fungicide, such as myclobutanil.

rusts and smuts

ANTIRRHINUM RUST

This seed-borne fungus (*Puccinia antirrhini*) spreads rapidly from plant to plant, often causing the plants to die.

Symptoms: Circles of blister-like pustules, full of dark brown spores, appear on the underside of the leaf, and yellow blotching is seen on the upper leaf surface. Leaves gradually wither and die, and the disease spreads to flowers and stems.

Plants attacked: Antirrhinums.

Prevention: Grow cultivars that offer some disease resistance, such as 'Monarch' and 'Royal Carpet Mixed'.

Control: Remove and burn infected plants. Apply a fungicide, such as flutriafol or mancozeb.

CHRYSANTHEMUM WHITE RUST

This fungus (*Puccinia horiana*) will attack plants growing indoors and outside. It usually overwinters on chrysanthemum stools or cuttings.

Symptoms: Cream-coloured (later light brown), blister-like pustules appear on the underside of the leaf, with yellow blotching on the upper surface. Leaves gradually become distorted and die.

Plants attacked: All types of chrysanthemum.

Prevention: Use only healthy plants for propagation. Avoid warm, humid conditions (in the greenhouse) and improve air circulation to check the development and spread of spores.

Control: Remove and burn infected plants. Apply a fungicide, such as mancozeb, to plants surrounding the infected plant.

DAHLIA SMUT

This fungus (*Entyloma calendulae* f. *dahliae*) lives in the soil and on plant debris. It usually starts to show only from midsummer onwards.

Symptoms: Pale brown spots with yellow margins, elongated in shape, fuse together to form large patches, spreading up from the lower leaves and gradually infecting the whole plant.

Plants attacked: Dahlias of all types are attacked by this fungus.

Prevention: Do not plant dahlias on an infected site for at least five years.

Control: Spray with Bordeaux mixture. Remove and burn badly infected plants. Drench the soil with cresylic acid. Remove all leaves and debris from tubers that are in storage.

PELARGONIUM RUST

This fungus (*Puccinia pelargonii-zonalis*) spreads rapidly from plant to plant, as spores drift in the air and germinate in moist conditions. The spores can survive for up to three years on dead leaves.

Symptoms: Concentric circles of blister-like pustules, full of dark brown spores, are seen on the underside of the leaf, with yellow blotching on the upper leaf surface. Leaves gradually wither and die. If the disease spreads unchecked the plants will die.

Plants attacked: All types of pelargonium, apart from ivy-leaved forms.

Prevention: Reduce humidity in greenhouses and conservatories and observe good hygiene, particularly clearing away infected fallen leaves. Allow more room between plants to improve air circulation.

Control: Remove and burn infected plants. Apply a fungicide, such as mancozeb.

ROSE RUST

This disease is caused by a fungus (*Phragmadium tuberculatum* or *P. mucronatum*) which penetrates the underside of the leaves, greatly weakening the plant and possibly eventually killing it.

Symptoms: Yellow blotches appear on the upper side of the leaves, with small, orange, blister-like structures, often arranged in rings, on the undersides. As the fungus spreads within the leaf it will gradually turn yellow and fall prematurely.

Plants affected: A wide range of plants suffer from rust, but this form is specific to roses.

Prevention: Grow resistant cultivars. Improve the circulation of air around individual plants.

Control: Remove and burn infected leaves and plants. Apply a fungicide, such as myclobutanil or mancozeb.

leaf spots and rots

BOX BLIGHT

This microfungus (*Cylindrocladium* spp.) is difficult to see with the naked eye. Box blight causes the total defoliation and death of infected plants within a month.

Symptoms: Groups of leaves turn brown, later straw coloured, with a layer of white felt on the underside of the leaf, before falling from the stem. Brownish-black streaks may be visible down the stems as they die.

Plants attacked: Box (*Buxus*) species and cultivars.

Prevention: Plant *B. microphylla* 'Faulkner', which shows some resistance.

Control: No control is available. Remove and burn infected material. Drench the soil with cresylic acid.

POTATO BLIGHT

This fungus (*Phytophthora infestans*) spreads in warm, humid conditions and can totally devastate a crop of potatoes, often destroying the tubers as well as the leaves and stems.

Symptoms: Dead patches develop on the leaves, starting from the margins and tip; the leaves wither and die as these spots spread. In humid conditions white mould forms on the undersides of the leaves. The stems gradually wither and die.

Plants attacked: Potatoes and tomatoes.

Prevention: Plant only healthy potato tubers. Grow resistant cultivars, such as 'Kondor', 'Cara', 'Estima', 'Record', 'Romano' and 'Maris Peer'.

Control: Spray with mancozeb or Bordeaux mixture when weather conditions favour the spread of blight spores.

RED THREAD

A spreading fungus (*Laetisaria fuciformis*; syn *Corticium fuciforme*), whose spores can often take two years to germinate. Grass leaves are always attacked but the roots can also be killed.

Symptoms: Patches of dying grass have a reddish tinge to the foliage, and fungal growths have red, needle-like structures coming from them.

Plants attacked: Turf, especially certain types of grass, including red fescues, bents and meadow grasses.

Prevention: Keep lawns well fed, especially in spring and summer or after heavy rain. Use resistant cultivars of lawn grass.

Control: Feed the lawn with a nitrogenous fertilizer to improve growth and vigour.

RHODODENDRON LEAF SPOT

Although this fungus (*Gloeosporium rhododendri*; syn. *Glomerella cingulata*) causes unsightly spots on the leaves of plants, it is only really damaging on plants that are unhealthy for another reason.

Symptoms: Purplish-black spots, often with distinctive black margins and clusters of black fruiting bodies in the centre of the spots, form on the leaves. A bad attack will cause the leaves to turn yellow and fall.

Plants attacked: Rhododendrons.

Prevention: Feed, water and mulch plants regularly to improve their health and vigour.

Control: Spray with myclobutanil. Rake up and burn up any fallen leaves.

ROSE BLACKSPOT

This fungal disease (*Diplocarpon rosae*) can cause the death of established roses if the attacks are repeated on a yearly basis. The disease overwinters on stem lesions, dormant buds and on fallen leaves or mulches.

Symptoms: Purplish-black spots form on the leaves and often spread, merging together, before the leaves turn yellow and fall from the plant. The disease may also develop on the stems.

Plants attacked: This disease is specific to all kinds of roses.

Prevention: Rake up and burn infected leaves. Spray the soil and plant with cresylic acid when the plants are dormant. Grow resistant cultivars if available.

Control: Spray with a suitable fungicide, such as myclobutanil or mancozeb, immediately after spring pruning.

PLANT PROBLEMS:
flowers and fruits

The problems that damage the flowers and fruits of your plants have a profound and noticeable effect, primarily because they ruin the 'end product' of your labours. A damaged flower looks unsightly and will not set seed as it should, reducing your crop next year. Damaged fruit may not reach maturity, and even if it does, may not be edible. It will rot quickly and may spread infection into the rest of the plant or into the other fruit being stored with it.

Many creatures are attracted to feed on buds and flowers, where the tissue is soft and succulent. They range from birds, such as the bullfinch, to insects and mites. Several insects are attracted to the blossom of trees and lay eggs that feed on and damage the developing fruitlets. The harm ranges from simply unsightly to highly dangerous to the well-being of the plant. Sometimes you might need to weigh the damage being caused against any possible benefit. The earwig, for instance, bites and chews flower petals, leaving them with ragged edges, but it also eats aphids.

The environment plays a part in several of the problems that affect flowers and fruit. Too much or too little water influences their development, and mineral deficiencies can cause distortion. Many of these problems can be averted altogether or corrected by establishing a regular routine of watering and feeding, by practising good hygiene (to deprive the pests of hiding places among fallen debris) and, where vegetables are concerned, by maintaining a proper rotation of crops so that one crop does not infect the next. The weather also plays its part in encouraging rots and moulds. Many fungi prefer moist conditions to grow and spread well, and you may find that your problems multiply in a warm, wet summer.

The early identification of a problem will help you treat it before it can spread too far. Infected vegetable plants can be removed and burned, but an ornamental shrub will need to be treated in situ. The damage to a rhododendron that shows the symptoms of bud blast (unopened buds dying and covered with black fungus) was probably caused by an earlier, unnoticed attack of rhododendron leafhoppers, which carry the spores of bud blast with them as they travel from plant to plant. In this instance, you will need to spray all your rhododendrons, not just the one showing signs of infection, because they are all equally likely to have been victims of the original insect attack.

Sadly, despite all your vigilance, there are some problems that simply do not become apparent until you bite into the fruit and find damaged flesh or a maggot inside. Using grease bands around the stems of fruit trees and giving the plants a precautionary spray when they are vulnerable at fruit-set will supplement constant vigilance. Make sure you buy new trees only from a reputable supplier, and seek out resistant varieties.

biting and burrowing pests

APPLE BLOSSOM WEEVIL

This weevil (*Anthonomus pomorum*) is about 6mm (¼in) long and has a brown body with white markings. It lays its eggs in the unopened flowers of apple trees.

Symptoms: Apple flowerbuds fail to develop and open, turning brown and gradually rotting. Inside the embryo blossom is a white grub, 7mm (¼in) long.

Plants attacked: Cropping and ornamental apples (*Malus*), both species and cultivars.

Prevention: There is no effective prevention method.

Control: If infestations were at high level the previous year, spray with bifenthrin just before the flower buds start to open. This should be done just before dusk to reduce the risk of spraying beneficial insects such as pollinating bees.

APPLE SAWFLY

These small, fly-like insects (*Hoplocampa testudinea*), which are about 1cm (½in) long, lay their eggs in the open blossoms in spring. They overwinter in the soil at the base of the tree.

Symptoms: Apple fruitlets drop from the tree prematurely. Inside these fruits a small white maggot, about 15mm (⅝in) long and with a brown head, feeds. Some fruits may develop with a brown corky scar around the skin.

Plants attacked: Most dessert apples; cooking apples are rarely attacked.

Prevention: Rake up and burn fallen fruitlets. Cultivate around the base of the tree in winter.

Control: Spray plants with bifenthrin within one week of petal fall.

BULLFINCHES

These small, colourful birds (*Pyrrhula pyrrhula*) feed on buds in cold weather to supplement their diet; each bullfinch can devour about 30 buds in an hour.

Symptoms: Long sections of branches are bare of flowerbuds or shoots in spring. This is due to birds pecking out the flowerbuds from late autumn through until late spring.

Plants attacked: Many plants are attacked, including apple (*Malus*), cherry and plum (*Prunus*), forsythia, gooseberry and pear (*Pyrus*).

Prevention: Place 25mm (1in) mesh netting over the trees as a protective barrier. Black cotton thread is also effective but it is time consuming to put up and take down.

Control: Bird scarers may have some effect on this problem.

CAPSID BUG

Small, pale green insects (*Lygus rugulipennis* and *Lygocoris pabulinus*) feed in the tips of shoots, and although the damage caused appears to be the result of biting, as these insects feed, they inject toxins into the plant tissue.

Symptoms: Flowers, leaves and shoots are distorted, often with many holes or tears in the plant tissue. The flowers have a ragged appearance. Fruits are badly distorted.

Plants attacked: A wide range, including apples (*Malus*), currants, gooseberries, raspberries and strawberries, as well as many ornamental plants.

Prevention: Practise good hygiene. Remove fallen plant debris and cultivate the soil around the base of the plants.

Control: Spray plants with bifenthrin at regular intervals from late spring.

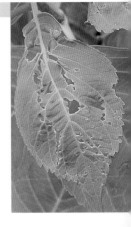

CODLING MOTH

This small moth (*Cydia pomonella*) lays its small translucent eggs on the fruits and leaves of apples (*Malus*) in midsummer.

Symptoms: The small, white caterpillars have a brown head. They burrow into the centre of the fruit, often causing it to fall prematurely.

Plants attacked: Apples and occasionally pears (*Pyrus*), medlar (*Mespilus*) and quince (*Cydonia*).

Prevention: Use pheromone insect traps to monitor the activity of the male moths.

Control: Spray twice with bifenthrin or an insecticide based on a plant extract, such as rape seed oil, at three-week intervals from midsummer (this is usually based on the number of adults caught in the pheromone trap).

EARWIGS

These fast-moving, small, shiny, brown insects (*Forficula auricularia*), up to 2.5cm (1in) long, have a pincer-like gripper on the tail.

Symptoms: Small circular notches or holes are eaten in the leaves and flowers of plants and vegetables.

Plants attacked: Herbacous perennials, especially chrysanthemums and dahlias, houseplants and young vegetables.

Prevention: A small amount of damage may be acceptable because earwigs also eat quite a number of aphids.

Control: Traps, such as straw-filled pots, can be used to catch the adult insects. Spray badly affected plants with bifenthrin.

PEA MOTH

Small moths (*Cydia nigricana*) appear from cocoons in the soil and fly on to pea plants to lay their eggs in midsummer.

Symptoms: Caterpillars, to 6mm (¼in) long, with creamy-white bodies, black markings and a black head, live inside the peapods and feed on the seeds as they develop.

Plants attacked: Peas of many types.

Prevention: Sow late and early crops to avoid the main egg-laying period. Cultivate the soil in winter to expose overwintering cocoons. Practise crop rotation.

Control: Spray caterpillars with bifenthrin one week after the first flowers open and repeat two weeks later.

PEAR MIDGE

This small, inconspicuous insect (*Contarinia pyrivora*) lays its eggs on the pear blossom after emerging from the soil in mid-spring.

Symptoms: Pear fruitlets start to turn black at the base within a few weeks of setting and fall from the tree. In the centre of the fruit is a pale orange maggot, about 3mm (⅛in) long.

Plants attacked: Fruiting and ornamental pears (*Pyrus*).

Prevention: Rake up and burn affected fruitlets.

Control: Spray adults with bifenthrin or an insecticide based on a plant extract, such as rape seed oil, at regular intervals from mid-spring.

PLUM MOTH

This moth (*Cydia funebrana*) lays small translucent eggs on the fruits and leaves of plums (*Prunus* spp.) in midsummer.

Symptoms: The fruit ripens prematurely and contains a small, pinkish-white or red caterpillar, about 12mm (½in) long, with a brown head. The flesh is eaten away around the stone, and fruits are often misshapen.

Plants attacked: Plums, damsons and greengages.

Prevention: Use pheromone insect traps to monitor the activity of the male moths.

Rake up and burn any fruit that has fallen prematurely.

Control: Spray twice with bifenthrin at three-week intervals from midsummer (this is usually based on the number of adults caught in the pheromone trap).

WINTER MOTH

The larvae of this insect (*Operophtera brumata*) are often first spotted when they have built 'shelters', which are groups of leaves loosely bound together with a silken thread to hide them from view.

Symptoms: Yellow-green caterpillars, to 25mm (1in) long, have paler lines running along their body. They feed on leaves, fruitlets and flowers, often causing the fruits to become misshapen as they develop.

Plants attacked: Most cropping fruit trees and many ornamental plants.

Prevention: Apply grease bands to the tree trunk in autumn to prevent the wingless females from climbing up to lay their eggs.

Control: Spray caterpillars with bifenthrin or an insecticide based on a plant extract, such as rape seed oil, at regular intervals.

DID YOU KNOW?

That it is possible to use combination planting to confuse certain pests. For example, you can mix onions and carrots together so that the aroma of the onions masks the scent of the carrots and confuses the carrot root fly and they fail to detect the carrots, leaving them alone. Unfortunately, for this to work, you need to plant six rows of onions to a single row of carrots.

rots and moulds

BITTER PIT

This disorder, sometimes known as apple bitter pit, is caused by a lack of available calcium in the soil. Young, rapidly growing trees bearing heavy crops are particularly susceptible, as are large-fruited cultivars, such as 'Bramley's Seedling' and 'Mutsu' ('Crispin').

Symptoms: Sunken brown markings are seen on the fruit. Small brown blotches in the flesh gradually merge as the fruit deteriorates. Fruits have a bitter taste even when ripe.

Plants attacked: Apples (*Malus domestica*).

Prevention: Keep plants well watered and well fed. Regularly check the nutritional status of plants.

Control: Spray the plants with a solution of calcium nitrate from early summer until early autumn.

BLOSSOM END ROT

This is a disorder, rather than a disease, which is caused by poor or erratic watering and a lack of available calcium in the soil or compost.

Symptoms: A sunken blackened patch develops at the base (flower end) of fruits as they mature. Not all fruits on the same plant will be affected.

Plants attacked: Tomatoes and peppers.

Prevention: Keep plants well watered and make sure there is sufficient calcium in the compost, particularly peat-based composts.

Control: Apply a solution of calcium chloride or calcium nitrate at 2g in 1 litre (2 pints) of water. Always try to water at the same times each day to reduce the fluctuation of water levels within the plant as much as possible.

BROWN ROT

This is a common and widespread fungal rot (*Sclerotinia fructigena*), which usually enters the fruit through small wounds and rots the fruit on the tree. These fruits become dried and 'mummified' but still release spores in humid conditions.

Symptoms: A soft brown rot on the skin and in the flesh of the fruit. As the rot develops, concentric rings of cream-coloured fungal blisters radiate out from the initial infection.

Plants attacked: Apples (*Malus*), peaches, nectarines, plums (*Prunus*), pears (*Pyrus*).

Prevention: Remove and burn all infected fruits.

Control: Apply a winter wash of cresylic acid when the plant is dormant.

BUD BLAST

The fungus (*Pycnostyanus azaleae*) invades the closed flowerbuds, causing them to rot. The disease is closely associated with the lifecycle of the rhododendron leafhopper (*Graphocephala fennabi*).

Symptoms: Flowerbuds remain closed, turning brown and hard, or 'mummified', on the stem. The bud gradually becomes covered in a layer of small, spiky fungal growths.

Plants attacked: Rhododendrons and azaleas.

Prevention: Spray with bifenthrin or an insecticide based on a plant extract, such as rape seed oil, to control the leafhoppers, which appear to carry the spores.

Control: Remove and burn infected buds.

COLOUR-BREAKING VIRUS

The disease shows up in many plants, but tulips are particularly susceptible to this type of infection, which is usually transmitted by sap-sucking insects, such as aphids.

Symptoms: Streaks of different colour in the flowers. Some flowers may be badly distorted or have dead (necrotic) patches in the flower. There may also be yellowing of the foliage and stunted growth.

Plants attacked: A wide range of plants is affected by a variety of different types of viruses and related, virus-like diseases.

Prevention: Grow white- and yellow-flowered cultivars, which do not appear to be affected.

Control: There is no control. Remove and burn infected plants as soon as they show symptoms.

GREY MOULD

This fungal mould (*Botrytis cinerea*) is possibly the most common disease seen in our gardens because it will live on a wide range of dead and living plant tissue. The spores are also able to lie dormant in the soil until a suitable host is present.

Symptoms: Greyish-white, furry mould spreads over infected decaying material, with spores drifting from the mouldy surface to cause further infection.

Plants attacked: Almost any plant, but particularly the soft tissue, such as flower petals and fruits.

Prevention: Remove any diseased or dead plant material. Keep the atmosphere as dry as possible.

Control: Spray with a suitable fungicide, such as green sulphur.

PETAL BLIGHT

This blight is also known as blossom wilt. The fungus *Sclerotinia laxa* enters through the flowers and leaves, killing them before spreading into the stems, often causing them to die back.

Symptoms: Shortly after appearing, flowers wilt and die, remaining withered on the shoots and often spreading spores to nearby leaves. Small, cream-coloured pustules may appear on the dead shoots.

Plants attacked: Cropping apples (*Malus domestica*), cherries (*Prunus cerasus* and *P. avium*) and pears (*Pyrus communis*), as well as their ornamental relatives; amelanchiers.

Prevention: Prune out infected flower trusses and dying shoots as soon as they are seen and burn them immediately.

Control: Spray with a copper-based fungicide just before the flowers open.

PYRACANTHA SCAB

The fungus *Spilocaea pyracanthae* infects the fruits and the leaves of the plant, making the leaves turn yellow. It is in these leaves and lesions on the stems and buds that the fungus survives from one year to the next.

Symptoms: Scabby patches, greyish-green to olive green in colour, spread over the berries, which stay small and fail to ripen, but split and fall prematurely.

Plants attacked: Pyracanthas.

Prevention: Grow resistant cultivars, such as 'Golden Charmer', 'Sappho Orange, 'Sappho Red' and 'Shawnee'. Remove yellow leaves from infected plants.

Control: Prune out badly affected shoots. Spray with myclobutanil.

STONY PIT

This virus affects the quality and flavour of the fruit and is usually transmitted when the plants are propagated, although it may take years to show.

Symptoms: Fruits become knobbly, dimpled and irregular in shape and size. Inside the fruits are many small 'gritty' particles in the flesh, which make them unpleasant to eat.

Plants attacked: Pears (*Pyrus*) and quince (*Cydonia*).

Prevention: Plant only certified stock (virus-free plants). Avoid certain cultivars, including 'Anjou', 'Doyenne du Comice', 'Laxton's Superb' and 'Winter Nelis', which are known to be susceptible to this virus.

Control: Remove and burn all infected plants to prevent the disease spreading to healthy trees.

SWEETCORN SMUT

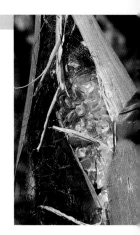

The fungus (*Ustilago maydis*) is spread either by wind-blown spores or by overwintering spores in the soil, and it is a greater problem in hot, dry seasons.

Symptoms: The cobs are swollen and distorted, and there is general stunting of the plant. Swellings are often a greyish-white colour and burst open to reveal masses of powdery brown spores.

Plants attacked: Sweetcorn, ornamental maize and forage maize.

Prevention: Remove and burn infected plant debris. Maintain good crop rotation.

Control: Remove and burn all infected plants before the spores are released to prevent the disease spreading to healthy plants.

DID YOU KNOW?

That research workers in the United States are developing an insecticide that has been extracted from a fungus which is in the same family as Clubroot, the fungus which attacks members of the cabbage family.

PLANT PROBLEMS:
stems

The causes of stem damage are wide-ranging but can be among the most directly harmful to the plant. Sap, the 'life-blood' of the plant, is carried within the main stem, which is also the support for all the growth above. If the stem is affected and weakened, the plant cannot function properly until it can repair the damage. If the damage is too severe, the plant will die. The most serious situation occurs where the entire stem has been circled, or 'girdled', by the attack, as this will usually interrupt the flow of sap up and down the stem. In this instance, the best you can do is cut the stem down to below the damage so that any buds at the base of the stem will develop into new shoots.

Bulbs have been included in this category because, botanically, a true bulb, such as *Narcissus*, is a compressed stem surrounded by modified leaves. Unless you regularly dig up the bulbs in your garden, you are unlikely to be aware of any attack until you see distorted growth or damaged flowers. At this point, it is important to identify the cause and treat it or dig up and remove the infected bulbs before the attack spreads.

Other infections, such as silver leaf in plums, may be hidden within the plant, so that the symptoms you see are the result of the infection rather than the attack itself. In this case, the first symptoms are seen on the roots, but the infection is in the stem.

Larger creatures can do a considerable amount of damage to your plants in a short space of time. If deer get into your garden they will graze on most non-woody plants (although they will also go for those too if the weather is bad), leaving jagged, torn wounds on the plants because they have no front teeth in their upper jaw and eat by gripping and pulling. Rabbits are slightly more selective, but equally destructive, particularly if you are growing vegetables. They even seem to prefer the flavour of apples being grown on dwarfing rootstocks over their larger counterparts.

Some of the smaller pests, like scale insects, are very well disguised and difficult to spot. They are camouflaged against the stem of the plant and only close inspection will reveal their presence. Wilting leaves and a 'failure to thrive' of one or more of the plant's shoots will often be the sign that makes you suspicious enough to check. Mealybug and woolly aphid are much easier to spot against the stem of the plant, as they are covered with a fluffy white coating, but this waxy coat also acts as protection to the pest and is difficult to penetrate with chemicals from the outside. For these creatures, a systemic insecticide, which acts on the pest as it sucks the sap, will be more effective.

As with every other type of attack, the key to success is to know your plants and be watchful for any change in growth or colour. The more quickly you spot the problem, the greater your chances of saving the plant.

sap-sucking pests

BROWN SCALE

These insects (*Parthenolecanium corni*) look like small brown blisters, 1–6mm (up to ¼in) long, on the stems and leaves of plants. They suck the sap, which gradually weakens the plants.

Symptoms: The plant's growth is stunted and distorted, and leaves gradually turn yellow. Plants become weak and susceptible to other pests and diseases. A sticky coating (honeydew) forms on lower leaves and is often accompanied by a black sooty mould on these leaves.

Plants attacked: Many ornamental plants, as well as conservatory and greenhouse plants.

Prevention: Place a layer of barrier glue around the stems of plants to stop the larval stage from moving into new sections of the plant.

Control: Introduce the parasitic wasp *Metaphycus helvolus*, the predator of scale insect, in midsummer. Apply sprays based on fatty acids in late spring and early summer, when the new scale insects (nymphs) are mobile.

MEALYBUG

These insects (*Pseudococcus* and *Planococcus* spp.) look like small, white, furry blisters, about 4mm (less than ¼in) long, on the stems and shoots of plants. They are capable of breeding all year round in a warm, humid environment.

Symptoms: There is stunted growth and a gradual decline as plants become weak and susceptible to other pests and diseases. A sticky coating (honeydew) forms on lower leaves and is often accompanied by a black sooty mould.

Plants attacked: Many ornamental plants, as well as conservatory and greenhouse plants.

Prevention: Keep newly introduced plants away from existing plants until you can be certain that they are pest free.

Control: Introduce the ladybird *Cryptolaemus montrouzieri* in summer, when the temperature is above 10°C (50°F). Apply sprays based on fatty acids or soft soap until late spring.

PEACH–POTATO APHID

These small, sap-sucking, winged and wingless insects (*Myzus persicae*) range in colour from pale green or yellow to pink. They are capable of transmitting viruses from one plant to another.
Symptoms: Shoot tips and young leaves are distorted. A sticky coating (honeydew) covers lower leaves and is often accompanied by a black sooty mould on these leaves.
Plants attacked: A wide range of plants, including trees, shrubs and climbers, and all vegetable and fruit crops.

Prevention: Remove and burn badly infected plants. Plant marigolds (*Tagetes* and *Calendula*) close to plants, as these attract hoverflies, which feed on aphids.
Control: Spray at regular intervals with bifenthrin as soon as the first aphids are seen in late spring.

STEM AND BULB EELWORM

These microscopic pests (*Ditylenchus dipsaci*), correctly called nematodes, live inside the plant. They move around on a film of moisture and are usually most active between spring and late summer.
Symptoms: Growth is weak and stunted, often with the shoot tips and young leaves being distorted. The leaves have brown, dead margins, and the bases on young plants are swollen. Later the stems thicken and rot. Many bulbous plants rot while they are in storage.

Plants attacked: A wide range of young plants, but particularly phlox and *Narcissus* bulbs, garlic and onions (*Allium*), and strawberries, any time from spring until late summer.
Prevention: Practise good crop rotation. Do not grow phlox, bulbs, potatoes or tomatoes on infected soil for at least six years.
Control: No chemical treatment is available to the amateur gardener. Remove and burn infected plants as soon as they are identified.

WOOLLY APHID

This sap-sucking pest (*Eriosoma lanigerum*) is present on its host plant throughout the year and can be difficult to eradicate because the woolly coating is a wax that sheds water-based sprays.
Symptoms: A fluffy, white, mould-like substance forms on the stems and branches around pruning cuts and on new shoots, where their feeding causes small, corky swellings to develop.
Plants attacked: Apples and crab apples (*Malus*), cotoneasters and pyracanthas.

Prevention: Spray dormant plants with tar acids every third year to kill off any overwintering insects. Cut out isolated infestations.
Control: Spray with derris (rotenone) in spring.

biting and chewing pests

DEER

Fallow deer (*Dama dama*), muntjac (*Muntiacus reevesi*) and roe deer (*Capreolus capreolus*) are the most likely to enter gardens and graze, with most of the feeding between dusk and dawn.
Symptoms: Stems, shoot tips and branches are eaten away, with a jagged wound left where the section of plant has been removed. This is because the deer feed by biting and tugging.
Plants attacked: Almost anything, but less likely to be woody plants, such as roses and shrubs.

Prevention: Consider growing plants such as *Pieris* spp., which have brightly coloured new shoots – the colour is said to deter grazing deer.
Control: Deterrents such as small bags of human hair suspended at the points where deer enter the garden have proved to be effective.

LEOPARD MOTH

This large insect (*Zeuzera pyrina*) lays eggs on the bark of trees, and the caterpillar eats into the stem, feeding for two years, reaching 55mm (2¼in) in length and creating a cavity within the stem.
Symptoms: The foliage may turn yellow, and there may be some shoot dieback. Stems sometimes snap to reveal a cavity in the stem at the point of breakage. A creamy-yellow caterpillar with many black spots may be seen.
Plants attacked: Trees, mainly apple (*Malus*), ash (*Fraxinus*), birch (*Betula*),

hawthorn (*Crataegus*), maple (*Acer*), oak (*Quercus*) and pears (*Pyrus*).
Prevention: No prevention is possible because attacks are localized and sporadic.
Control: Insert a section of wire into the cavity to skewer the caterpillar.

RABBITS

Rabbits (*Oryctolagus cuniculus*) eat about 0.5kg (more than 1lb) of plant material each a day, and a few can devastate a garden in a short period of time.

Symptoms: In winter bark is chewed away from trees to a height of about 45cm (18in), leaving the wood beneath exposed. If the stem is girdled, the tree will come into growth the following spring before the top (above the wound) dies.

Plants attacked: A wide range of trees, mainly young ones and particularly apple (*Malus*) and its relatives.

Prevention: Wire or plastic tree guards, to 60cm (24in) high, can be wrapped around the stem to protect the tree bark.

Control: Erect rabbit-proof fencing around the boundary.

ROSE GALL WASP

A small wasp (*Diplolepis rosae*) lays its eggs in buds along the stem in summer, and these mossy growths are created as a result of the feeding activity of the grubs inside.

Symptoms: Spherical, orange-green galls, up to 6cm (2½in) across, with a mossy appearance, develop on the stems. These are caused by many small white grubs feeding in the woody centre of the gall.

Plants attacked: Wild and cultivated roses of all types.

Prevention: There is no effective prevention.

Control: The galls appear to do no physical harm to the plant, but they look unsightly. Remove and burn affected stems and shoots.

SLUGS

Slugs are slimy, with tubular-shaped bodies, up to 10cm (4in) long, and range in colour from creamy-white through grey to jet black.

Symptoms: As slugs feed they make circular holes in the plant tissue, often causing extensive cavities. Damaged seedlings are usually killed. Attacks generally take place at night.

Plants attacked: A wide range of plants, including hostas, herbaceous perennials, seedlings and food crops, will be damaged on any part of the plant they can reach. Slugs are more of a problem on wet sites and clay soils.

Prevention: Keep the soil well drained and weed free. Remove all plant debris. Apply the pathogenic nematode (*Phasmarhabditis hermaphrodita*) when the soil temperature rises above 5°C (41°F).

Control: Apply aluminium sulphate or metaldehyde in spring as the eggs hatch around the base of plants.

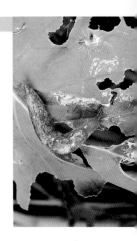

cankers and wilts

APPLE CANKER

A fungus (*Nectria galligena*) causes swellings and distorted growths on the stems of plants. This is followed by the death of the branch or stem, as the fungus eventually girdles it.

Symptoms: There are open wounds (some weeping), uneven scar tissue, irregular stem development or large, corky-textured swellings, mainly on woody tissue.

Plants affected: A wide range of plants, including apple (*Malus*), beech (*Fagus*), hawthorn (*Crataegus*), pears (*Pyrus*), poplar (*Populus*), *Sorbus* and willow (*Salix*).

Prevention: Take care not to damage plants when pruning. Improve the drainage. Purchase new plants from a reliable nursery or garden centre.

Control: Remove and burn infected branches. Clean and paint over open wounds with a proprietary wound paint.

CORAL SPOT

This common fungus (*Nectria cinnabarina*) usually gains entry through any dead wood of plants but will later invade the live growing tissue.

Symptoms: Individual branches wilt in summer, and grey-brown staining may be found under the bark of infected shoots. In autumn these dead branches will be covered in small, salmon pink, blister-like marks.

Plants attacked: A wide range of woody plants, including Japanese maples (*Acer palmatum*), magnolias, mulberries (*Morus*), pyracanthas and walnuts (*Juglans*).

Prevention: Prune in summer when there are no fungal spores being released into the air. Do not leave old dead prunings lying around.

Control: Remove and burn infected material as quickly as possible.

DUTCH ELM DISEASE

This disease is caused by a fungus (*Ophiostoma ulmi*, syn. *Ceratocystis ulmi*), which blocks the tree's vascular system, leading to wilting and death. The disease is transmitted by the elm bark beetle (*Scolytus scolytus*) and the small elm bark beetle (*S. multistriatus*) as they feed on the young shoots of elm (*Ulmus*).

Symptoms: New shoots show signs of wilting at the tips, which curl downwards to form a 'shepherd's crook'. Leaves turn yellow, before turning brown and dying. There is progressive dieback down the whole tree. The bark of the tree will flake away, revealing the feeding galleries of the elm beetle grubs.

Plants attacked: Many elms (*Ulmus*) and *Zelkova* spp.

Prevention: Some hybrids of Asian elms, such as *Ulmus* 'Sapporo Autumn Gold', and the species *U. laevis* appear to be resistant to the disease.

Control: At present there is no effective chemical control for this disease.

FIREBLIGHT

Fireblight is a disease that is caused by bacteria (*Erwinia amylovora*), which move on a film of water, invading the soft tissue of plants and eventually killing them.

Symptoms: Flowers and young shoots become blackened and shrivelled. Leaves wilt and turn brown, and shoots die back as the disease progresses. Plants eventually die.

Plants attacked: Many members of the rose family (Rosaceae), including cotoneasters, crab apple (*Malus*), hawthorn (*Crataegus*), pyracanthas, *Sorbus* and quince (*Cydonia*).

Prevention: Grow as few susceptible plants as possible. Avoid growing late-flowering cultivars of apple, which are more susceptible to attack.

Control: Remove and burn any plants with the above symptoms. Disinfect pruning tools after use. In parts of Britain this is a notifiable disease, and the Department for Environment, Farming and Rural Affairs (DEFRA) should be informed of any outbreak.

SILVER LEAF

The fungus (*Chondrostereum purpureum*) enters the woody tissue of members of the *Prunus* genus, usually when the plant is dormant.

Symptoms: Leaves of infected trees adopt a silvery sheen, and branches die back until the whole plant eventually succumbs. As the tree dies, brownish-purple, spore-bearing fungal brackets appear on branches and stems.

Plants attacked: Any relative of *Prunus*, both ornamental and fruiting, that has just been pruned may become infected and killed. Poplars (*Populus*) may also be attacked.

Prevention: Prune in summer when there are no fungal spores being released into the air.

Control: Prune infected branches from healthy trees, cutting back by at least 15cm (6in) into healthy wood. Badly infected trees must be removed and burned.

galls and witches' brooms

AZALEA GALL

A fungus (*Exobasidium vaccinii*) produces spores that are carried on the wind and by insects to infect healthy plants. The symptoms may not show for several months after infection.

Symptoms: Swollen, irregular growths form on stem tips, leaves and occasionally petals, varying in colour from pale green to pinkish-red. These later turn white as a layer of spores is formed on their surface.

Plants attacked: Indoor rhododendrons and azaleas as well as outdoor azaleas.

Prevention: Provide good ventilation and low humidity. Do not propagate from infected plants.

Control: Remove and burn the galls before they turn white and shed their spores.

CROWN GALL

Crown gall is caused by a bacterium (*Agrobacterium tumefaciens*), is common and widespread on a range of plants, and in mild cases often goes unnoticed.

Symptoms: Irregular, spherical growths are seen on stems and branches; they are hard, woody and spiky on trees and shrubs, and soft and fleshy on herbaceous plants, often rotting later. Plants may show a reduction in growth and vigour.

Plants attacked: Many, including fruit, vegetables and both woody and herbaceous ornamental plants.

Prevention: Bacteria may be present in the soil and may or may not invade plant tissue, so prevention is not possible.

Control: Remove and burn branches and stems with signs of swollen, gall-like structures.

FASCIATION

Irregular growth, usually as a result of uneven cell division in the stem, may be caused by bacterial attack, insect activity within the stem or genetic mutation.

Symptoms: Growth is twisted or flattened, often appearing as many stems joined together. Leaves may be grouped together in clusters. There may be large swellings on the trunks of trees.

Plants attacked: Almost any plant can show symptoms, but it is more noticeable on woody subjects.

Prevention: None. Some plants are actually grown for their distorted growth – *Salix udensis* 'Sekka' (syn. *S.* 'Setsuka'), for example. Some plants with the cultivar name 'Contorta', such as *Corylus avellana* 'Contorta', may even be plants propagated to retain this fasciated growth.

Control: Prune out distorted growths by removing complete stems and shoots if possible.

PINEAPPLE GALL

A small, sap-sucking insect (*Adelges abietis*) feeds on the buds of conifers in spring and produces chemicals that distort the shoot tips.

Symptoms: Swollen shoot tips resemble miniature green pineapples, with young insects inside them. These turn brown and release the insects. The activity of this pest may lead to large numbers of leaves ('needles') being shed from the branches leaving long, unsightly sections of bare wood visible. It is unusual for the leaves to re-grow on these sections.

Plants attacked: Norway spruce (*Picea abies*) and many other species of spruce.

Prevention: Keep plants well watered. Spray the foliage with water in summer.

Control: Spray with a contact or systemic insecticide between late autumn and early spring before egg-laying starts.

WITCHES' BROOMS

These strange growth clusters are usually caused by fungal activity, particularly *Taphrina* spp., or occasionally by mites feeding on branches, causing localized cell disruption.

Symptoms: Clusters of dense, twiggy growth, looking rather like a bird's nest on tree branches; these are usually noticed in the winter after leaf fall.

Plants attacked: Acacia, birch (*Betula*), cherry and plum (*Prunus*) and hornbeam (*Carpinus*) are regularly seen bearing witches' brooms, but other plants may also carry them.

Prevention: There is no prevention for this problem.

Control: Remove and burn affected branches; they are, in fact, often left as they do no apparent harm to the host plant.

PLANT PROBLEMS:
roots

The biggest single difficulty about an attack on the roots of a plant is that you seldom realize it is happening until it is too late. No one routinely digs up their plants to do a health check, so unless something makes you suspicious, the attack is well under way before you even realize it's there.

The attack may be from any one of a number of sources. It may be a pest actually chewing or sucking at the roots or tunnelling alongside them and causing them to lose contact with the surrounding soil. Alternatively, it may be a fungus or bacterial rot that invades the plant from within the soil, causing gradual weakening and, finally, death. Whichever causes the original damage, the plant is likely to be seriously weakened and can be left with open wounds, which encourage further attack by secondary infections. These are usually present in the soil all the time, but do no harm unless they are presented with an open door through which to enter the plant's system.

When the attack is above ground you will notice signs, such as chewed or discoloured leaves, clusters of feeding insects or distorted growth, that will give you early warning that action needs to be taken. The first you know of a root attack is usually when the plant wilts and dies. This is where it really does pay to know your plants, so that you can recognize that something is going wrong. Pale, dull foliage, small flowers or buds being shed before they open can act as indicators that all is not right. A general 'failure to thrive' can often be taken as a strong hint that you should probably investigate below ground to see what is happening. If the plant is healthy and free from infection, it can be replanted, watered and fed, and the worst it should suffer is a check in growth. However, if it is infected, it will need treating and quite possibly isolating until you can deal with the problem.

A healthy plant is much better able to cope with an attack by any pest or disease than one that is already under stress for another reason, such as erratic watering. For this reason it is always important to practise good techniques in the garden. Water, feed and examine your plants regularly, and make sure that you tidy up after yourself when you are working, removing any debris you might have created before it can attract disease. Use clean, sterile compost when you are growing seedlings or cuttings and put them in trays or pots that have been given a thorough wash in a cleaning solution. When you buy new plants, get them from a reputable source, and if you are aware of a previous problem, look for resistant varieties, as the range is increasing all the time and presents much less of a barrier to growing plants than it used to. Most importantly, if you suspect an attack has begun, try to identify and treat it as soon as you possibly can. The earlier it is dealt with, the more likely that you will save the plant.

sap-sucking pests

ROOT APHIDS

Several species of these aphids, up to 3mm (⅛in) long and varying in colour from creamy-brown to bluish-green, live on the roots of garden plants, feeding by sucking sap.

Symptoms: A general reduction in the growth rate of plants as well as wilting in sunny weather, even though the soil is moist. Exposed roots show the white, waxy protective coat the aphids produce.

Plants attacked: Auriculas and roses; French and runner beans, Jerusalem artichokes and lettuce.

Prevention: Where possible, remove and burn infected plants. Controlling ants in the garden can help, because they often protect this pest and harvest its honeydew.

Control: These are harder to control than other aphids. Use an insecticide containing derris as a drench. Use chemical formulations based on imidacloprid for non-edible plants only. Drench newly transplanted plants with a solution of armillatox.

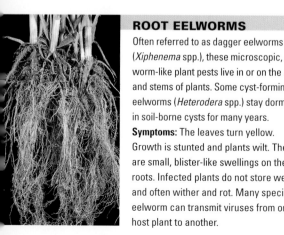

ROOT EELWORMS

Often referred to as dagger eelworms (*Xiphenema* spp.), these microscopic, worm-like plant pests live in or on the roots and stems of plants. Some cyst-forming eelworms (*Heterodera* spp.) stay dormant in soil-borne cysts for many years.

Symptoms: The leaves turn yellow. Growth is stunted and plants wilt. There are small, blister-like swellings on the roots. Infected plants do not store well and often wither and rot. Many species of eelworm can transmit viruses from one host plant to another.

Plants attacked: Many vegetables and ornamental plants, including brassicas, carrots, onions, peas, potatoes and tomatoes, and figs (*Ficus*).

Prevention: Grow resistant cultivars. Provide good drainage. Practise crop rotation, leaving a minimum of seven or eight years between crops to allow the soil-borne population to die out.

Control: Remove and burn any plants with the above symptoms.

ROOT KNOT EELWORMS

These 1mm long, worm-like plant pests (*Meloidogyne* spp.) live in the roots of plants. A single female can lay up to 500 eggs in a month.

Symptoms: The foliage is often dull or pale green. Growth is distorted and stunted, and plants wilt. Small, knobbly swellings can be seen on the roots. Infected plants do not store well and often wither and rot.

Plants attacked: Plants growing in greenhouses or in light sandy soils, especially chrysanthemums and cyclamen; carrots, onions, potatoes and tomatoes.

Prevention: Grow resistant cultivars. Improve the drainage. Practise correct crop rotation. Use growing bags or raised beds in the greenhouse.

Control: Remove and burn any plants with the above symptoms.

ROOT MEALYBUGS

Small, 2–3mm (⅛in) long, flat insects (*Rhizoecus* spp.), which are covered in a white woolly substance, live on the roots of plants.

Symptoms: There is a general lack of vigour and an overall reduction in plant growth. Plants are susceptible to attack from other pests and diseases.

Plants attacked: Mostly container-grown plants in fairly dry, free-draining compost mixes or where watering is erratic, including African violets (*Saintpaulia*), cacti, fuchsias and pelargoniums.

Prevention: Keep plants well watered. Remove and destroy any suspect plants. Controlling ants in the garden can help, because they often protect this pest and harvest its honeydew.

Control: Where possible, use chemical formulations based on imidacloprid as a drench or spray.

DID YOU KNOW?

That rotenone, the main insecticidal constituent of derris, is extracted from the roots of *Derris* and *Lonchocarpus* plants and is harmful to bees and fish.

biting and chewing pests

CABBAGE ROOT FLY

The small fly (*Delia radicum*) lays eggs 5–7cm (2–3in) from host plants, and, as the eggs hatch, white grubs, about 8mm (⅓in) long, feed on the roots.

Symptoms: The outer leaves of attacked plants show signs of wilting, even in moist soil, and these leaves first turn a dull green before taking on a bluish-orange sheen. Plants have most of their finer roots eaten away. With radish, swede and turnip, feeding occurs inside the main root.

Plants attacked: Any member of the Brassicaceae family, vegetables as well as ornamental plants, including alyssum, aubrietas, stocks (*Matthiola*) and wallflowers (*Erysimum*).

Prevention: Cut down any hedge parsley (*Anthriscus sylvestris*) before it flowers, because the females feed on this before laying their eggs.

Control: Place 10cm (4in) diameter cardboard or felt discs around the base of plants. The eggs are laid on the discs, where they dry out and die. Use an insecticide containing derris as a drench.

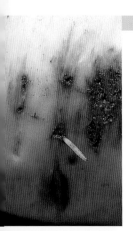

CARROT ROOT FLY

This is a serious pest of carrots and other umbelliferous crops. The small fly (*Psila rosae*) lays eggs close to host plants, and, as the eggs hatch, slender creamy-white grubs, about 1cm (⅓in) long, feed on the roots.

Symptoms: Growth is stunted. Leaves redden, and rusty-brown lines can be seen on the outside of the tap roots where the feeding tunnels have collapsed. The open wounds make the roots susceptible to fungal and bacterial rots; attacked roots do not usually survive well in storage.

Plants attacked: Celery, celeriac, carrot, fennel, parsley and parsnips.

Prevention: Covering the young plants with horticultural fleece will prevent the females from laying eggs close to the plants. Grow resistant cultivars, such as 'Flyaway'. 'Parano' or 'Sytan'.

Control: Sowing after late spring will avoid the first generation of larvae. Carrots harvested before late summer will miss the second generation. Use an insecticide containing derris as a drench.

CHAFER GRUBS

The larva of the garden chafer (*Phyllopertha horticola*) has a brown head and creamy-white body with three pairs of legs. It often curls into a C-shape.

Symptoms: Plants suddenly collapse as the pest eats through the roots of young plants and turf grasses just below soil level, often causing yellow patches on lawns.

Plants attacked: Lawns, young bedding and ornamental plants and vegetable plants.

Prevention: They prefer light, free-draining soils and are often hunted by foxes and badgers, which dig holes in lawns.

Control: Treat the soil around susceptible plants with the parasitic nematode *Steinernema carpocapsae*, which parasitizes and kills the pest. Use an insecticide containing derris as a drench.

LEATHERJACKETS

The grey-brown, tubular-shaped, wrinkled-skinned larvae of craneflies (*Tipula paludosa*) are up to 45mm (1¾in) long. They live and feed in the soil until early autumn, before emerging as adults.

Symptoms: The larvae eat through the roots and sometimes stems of young vegetable plants and turf grasses just below soil level, often causing yellow patches on lawns.

Plants attacked: A wide range of young plants, including bedding plants, pot plants and turf grasses.

Prevention: Keep the soil well-drained. Dig over the ground in early autumn, especially if it has been fallow throughout summer.

Control: Water the soil or lawn and cover with black plastic or tarpaulin overnight; the larvae will work their way to the surface and can be exposed for the birds to eat the following day. In the mid- to late summer apply the pathogenic nematode *Steinernema carpocapsae* as a biological control to parasatize the larvae.

ONION FLY

Maggots of *Delia antiqua*, creamy-white in colour up to 8mm (⅜in) long.

Symptoms: This pest eats through the roots and stems of young vegetable plants just below soil level, causing plants to wilt and die. If the attack occurs late in the season, the main damage is often caused to the bulbs as they are eaten and start to rot in storage.

Plants attacked: Young vegetable plants, particularly garlic, leek, onion and shallot.

Prevention: Grow onions from sets, good crop rotations, and hoe soil surface regularly. Planting parsley amongst the susceptible plants will help to deter the pest.

Control: Treat the soil around susceptible plants with derris applied as a dust in early to mid summer.

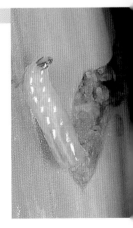

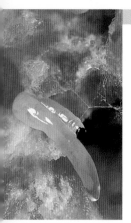

SCIARID FLY

Small brownish-grey flies (fungus gnats; *Bradysia paupera*), up to 4mm (¼in) long, with slender bodies, lay eggs in compost (especially peat-based compost) in which indoor plants are growing.
Symptoms: Small, transparent, black-headed maggots, up to 5mm long (¼in), feed on decaying organic matter and the thin young roots of plants, causing wilting and rotting at the base of the plant.
Plants attacked: A wide range of indoor tender plants, bedding plants and cuttings.

Prevention: Keep compost well-drained.
Control: Spray adults with an insecticide based on fatty acid or rape seed oil. Hang up yellow sticky traps to catch adults.

SYMPHYLIDS

Garden symphylids, sometimes called symphylans (*Scutigerella immaculata*), have thin, white bodies with 12 pairs of legs and long antennae. Symphylids are about 1cm (½in) long and live for up to a year in the soil or compost. They are found mainly in greenhouses.
Symptoms: Holes are seen in the roots and tubers of plants, often causing the above-ground parts to collapse. Seedlings attacked by symphylids are usually killed.

Plants attacked: A wide range of plants, including, bulbs, bedding, vegetables and seedlings.
Prevention: None; see below.
Control: There is no effective control other than good crop hygiene.

VINE WEEVIL

A white, legless grub (*Otiorhynchus sulcatus*) with a black or dark brown head, usually curled into a C-shape, feeds on the roots of plants. The adults (female only) are about 9mm (⅓in) long.
Symptoms: Plants wilt or totally collapse; when examined, most of the roots are missing from affected plants. Small, semicircular notches are bitten out of the leaf margins by the adult weevil.
Plants attacked: A wide range of plants, including begonias, camellias, cyclamen, fuchsias, primulas and rhododendrons.

Prevention: Avoid crocking containers and keep the soil clear of debris and litter, which offers hiding places for adult female insects. Cover the soil or compost with a layer of grit to deter egg laying.
Control: Treat the soil around susceptible plants with parasitic nematodes (*Heterorhabditis megidis* and *Steinernema carpocapsae*), which parasitize and kill the pest. Use chemical formulations based on imidacloprid or drench containers with armillatox solution. Grow plants in compost treated with fipronil.

WIREWORMS

Thin, yellow bodies (looking rather like pieces of fresh straw), pointed at each end and about 3cm (1¼in) long, are the larvae of the garden click beetle (skipjack; *Athous haemorrhoidalis* and *Agriotes* spp.). The larvae feed in the soil for four or five years before becoming adults.

Symptoms: Holes in the roots and tubers of plants often cause the above-ground parts to collapse. Attacked seedlings are usually killed.

Plants attacked: A wide range of plants, including bulbs, bedding plants, vegetables and seedlings. They are serious pests of cereals (wheat, barley and oats).

Prevention: Avoid planting susceptible plants for up to three years on soil that has recently been grassland or left uncultivated.

Control: Grow small patches of wheat or mustard in the garden to attract the wireworms to the roots, dig up the plants and leave the larvae for the birds. Apply derris as a drench.

WOODLICE

Small, greyish-brown, scale-like creatures (*Oniscus asellus*, *Armadillidium vulgare* and others), up to 15mm (⅝in) long, have segmented shells and curl into balls when disturbed.

Symptoms: Roots and the base of stems are chewed through, causing plants to wilt and collapse. Injury may also lead to rotting at the base of the plant.

Plants attacked: A wide range of plants, but mainly seedlings of vegetables and bedding plants.

Prevention: Sterilize pots and seed trays, and keep soil and compost as dry as possible (woodlice must have humid conditions).

Control: Dust hiding sites under stones and the like with an insecticide containing bendiocarb.

DID YOU KNOW?

That in recent years two new species of vine weevil, which are pests in southern Europe, have been discovered feeding on plants in London. Armadillo weevil (*Otiorhynchus armadillo*) and willow weevil (*Otiorhynchus salicicola*) are both larger and paler in colour than the northern European native vine weevil (*Otiorhynchus sulcatus*).

rots

FAIRY RINGS

Soil-borne fungi (*Marasmius oreades*) feed on organic matter and grass roots in the soil.

Symptoms: Two dark circles of lush grass form, with the area between containing only dead grass and moss. Light brown toadstools may appear in autumn on the outer ring of grass.

Plants attacked: Fine quality turf grasses, especially in intensively managed lawns.

Prevention: Remove as much organic matter and debris as possible when preparing the ground for a lawn.

Control: Applying a dilute solution of cresylic acid to the infected area and for at least 60cm (24in) around the infection may provide some control.

GIANT POLYPORE

The fungus (*Meripilus giganteus*) is one of the most common causes of root rot and death in mature trees, although it usually takes several years after infection before death occurs. Trees may become unstable before any obvious symptoms are visible.

Symptoms: The foliage is sparse and pale green. Blackened, rotting roots and pale brown bracket fungi emerge from around the roots at the base of the trunk.

Plants attacked: A wide range of trees, particularly beech (*Fagus*), birch (*Betula*), oak (*Quercus*) and sweet chestnut (*Castanea sativa*).

Prevention: Inspect mature trees regularly. Prune in spring and early summer.

Control: Remove and burn infected material. Drench the soil with a dilute solution of cresylic acid.

HONEY FUNGUS

This aggressive, soil-borne fungus (*Armillaria* spp.) produces honey-coloured, umbrella-shaped toadstools in autumn.

Symptoms: Many plants appear to be suffering from drought but also exhibit premature leaf fall, dead branches and twigs. Large pieces of bark fall from the wood. The plant dies.

Plants attacked: A wide range of plants, including many trees, shrubs and herbaceous perennials.

Prevention: Do not grow susceptible plants, such as birch (*Betula*), cypress (*Cupressus*), Leyland cypress (x *Cupressocyparis leylandii*), willow (*Salix*) and wisteria.

Control: There is no truly effective control. Dig up and burn infected plants as soon as the disease is confirmed.

ONION WHITE ROT

A soil-borne fungus (*Sclerotium cepivorum*) causes the collapse and death of onions and related plants.

Symptoms: The leaves turn yellow, and the plant collapses as the roots rot. Dense, white felty growth appears around the base of the bulb and on the roots.

Plants attacked: Chives, garlic, leeks, salad onions and shallots.

Prevention: Grow the resistant onion cultivar 'Norstar'. Practise good crop rotation (the fungal spores can survive for up to seven years in the soil). Do not work on contaminated plots before working on non-contaminated areas.

Control: Remove and burn infected plants as soon as they are identified.

PHYTOPHTHORA ROOT DEATH

This is caused by many different species of *Phytophthora*, a fungus that invades and kills a wide range of woody plants.

Symptoms: The foliage is sparse and discoloured. The stem dies back, and the whole plant eventually dies. Roots show a blackish-brown discoloration, which spreads up into the stem. The dead bark falls away from the roots and stems.

Plants attacked: Apple (*Malus*), beech (*Fagus*), cherries (*Prunus*), cypress (*Cupressus*), lime (*Tilia*), rhododendron and yew (*Taxus*); many ornamental plants can also be attacked.

Prevention: Keep soil well drained because the disease is much worse in waterlogged conditions.

Control: Remove and burn infected material. Drench the soil with cresylic acid, although there is no specific fungicide available to amateur gardeners to deal with this fungus.

POTATO BLACKLEG

This rot is caused by a bacterium (*Erwinia carotovora*), which is carried on diseased tubers and spreads rapidly through moist soil, especially in the spring.

Symptom: The leaves are yellow and curled, and growth is stunted. The roots, tubers and base of the stem are black and rotten, often slimy and falling apart.

Plants attacked: Potatoes; also possibly weeds belonging to the potato family, such as black nightshade (*Solanum nigrum*).

Prevention: Keep the soil well drained. Discard any tubers that show signs of blackening or discoloration.

Control: Remove and burn infected plants. Grow the cultivar 'Saxon', which appears to show some resistance to the disease.

SCLEROTINIA DISEASE

This disease is caused by a fungus (*Sclerotinia sclerotiorum*), which invades roots and causes rotting. Spores can lie dormant in the soil for up to five years.

Symptoms: The leaves are yellow. The plant will collapse as roots form a soft, brown rot, showing as a dense, white, felty growth around the base of the stem and on the roots.

Plants attacked: A wide range, including herbaceous perennials, chrysanthemums, dahlias and many vegetables.

Prevention: Keep soil weed free because the fungus may survive on weeds until crops or ornamental plants are introduced.

Control: Remove and burn infected plants. Check stored root vegetables regularly for wet, rotting patches.

STRAWBERRY RED CORE

Strawberry red core (*Phytophthora fragariae*) is a soil-borne fungus that destroys strawberry plants by invading the roots. The fungal spores can survive for up to 12 years in the soil.

Symptoms: In late spring strawberry plants show signs of stunted growth. Leaves become tinged red and brown. Roots are discoloured and rotting, with the centre stained reddish-pink.

Plants attacked: Strawberries (*Fragaria* spp.) only.

Prevention: Keep the soil well-drained and grow plants on ridges to prevent their roots becoming waterlogged.

Control: Remove and burn infected plants. Apply a dilute solution of cresylic acid to the infected area and at least 60cm (24in) around the infection, as this may provide some control.

VIOLET ROOT ROT

Violet root rot is a soil-borne fungus (*Helicobasidium purpureum*) that invades and kills the host plants. It is a particular problem when the soil is warm and above 15°C (59°F).

Symptoms: Plants appear weak and stunted, with yellow blotching on the leaves. The roots and base of the plant, especially bulbs, corms and rhizomes, are often covered with a greyish-purple, felt-like coating.

Plants attacked: Asparagus, beetroot, carrots, celery, parsnips, potatoes, swedes and turnips; many herbaceous perennials.

Prevention: Improve soil drainage. Add lime to the soil because this disease is more prevalent on acid soils.

Control: Remove and burn infected plants. Drench the soil around infected plants with a product based on tar acids or with a copper-based fungicide.

WHITE ROOT ROT

This common and widespread disease is caused by a fungus (*Rosellinia necatrix*), which attacks the roots of a wide range of plants, especially on poorly drained soils.

Symptoms: Plants show reduced growth and vigour, and leaves turn yellow. The plants wilt and collapse as the roots rot. Dense, white felty growth is seen around the base of the affected plant as well as on the roots.

Plants attacked: A wide range, including grape vine (*Vitis vinifera*), apple (*Malus*), pears (*Pyrus*), potato, flower bulbs and privet (*Ligustrum*).

Prevention: Improve the drainage of the soil.

Control: Remove and burn infected plants. Dig over the soil to expose as much of the fungus as possible (it is susceptible to drying out and dies).

DID YOU KNOW?

That many fungal diseases that attack the roots of plants are present in the soil all of the time, but only become a problem when plants are stressed by incidents such as waterlogging or drought, making them more vulnerable to attack.

wilts

CARNATION WILT

The soil-borne fungus (*Fusarium oxysporum* f. *dianthi*) is present in the soil in plant debris and usually builds up to dangerous levels when the same plants are grown in the same soil on a regular basis.

Symptoms: The leaves and stems wilt. Reddish-purple patches develop on leaves and stems; these areas may be a greyish-yellow as the plant dies. Dark staining is seen in the roots and lower stem. Plants wilt during the day but recover at night.

Plants attacked: Carnations and pinks (*Dianthus* cvs).

Prevention: Practise good crop rotation. Use only healthy plants for propagation. Improve soil drainage.

Control: Remove and burn infected plants and any contaminated soil.

CLUBROOT

The primitive fungus (*Plasmodiophora brassicae*) spreads through the soil on a film of water and can remain in the ground for over 20 years, particularly if it is a wet, acidic soil.

Symptoms: The plant's leaves and stems turn pale green or even yellow, with pinkish markings. Frequent wilting occurs, even when the soil is moist, although the plant appears to recover. The roots become swollen and distorted, with lumpy swellings.

Plants attacked: All members of the cabbage family (Brassicaceae) and its relatives.

Prevention: Improving drainage and adding lime to the soil can greatly reduce the risk of infection. Grow resistant cultivars of vegetables.

Control: Dip the roots of young transplants in a preparation of thiophanate-methyl before transplanting.

PANSY SICKNESS

The soil-borne fungus (*Pythium violae*) is present in the soil in plant debris and usually builds up to dangerous levels when the same plants are grown in the same soil on a regular basis.

Symptoms: The whole plant wilts and collapses. The foliage turns yellow as the plant dies over a period of several weeks.

Plants attacked: Pansies and violas.

Prevention: Practise good crop rotation. Use only healthy plants for propagation.

Control: Remove and burn infected plants. Apply a dilute solution of cresylic acid to the infected area, as this may provide some control. For beds which are used regularly, it may be worth considering replacing the soil to a depth of 1ft (30cm) every 3–4 years.

PEA WILT

The soil-borne fungus (*Fusarium oxysporum* f. *pisi*) is present in the soil and builds up in the ground when peas or its relatives are grown in the same soil on a regular basis.

Symptoms: The leaves and stems wilt rapidly, turning yellow before dying. Plants often wilt during the day but recover at night. Dark brown staining can be seen in the roots and lower stem.

Plants attacked: Peas and close relatives, including sweet peas (*Lathyrus*).

Prevention: Practise good crop rotation. Use only healthy plants for propagation. Improve soil drainage. Grow resistant pea cultivars, such as 'Kelvedon', 'Onward' and 'Greenshaft'.

Control: Remove and burn infected plants. Apply a dilute solution of cresylic acid to the infected area, as this may provide some control.

DID YOU KNOW?

When rabbits and hares eat the bark of trees in a cold winter, they select the plants that have the highest sugar content in the bark and eat those first.

PELARGONIUM BLACKLEG

The fungus (*Pythium* spp.) lives in dirty compost and pots and thrives in poorly ventilated, humid greenhouses.

Symptoms: The leaves turn yellow, wilt and die, while a blackening progresses up the stems from the roots or base of cuttings. The stem becomes shrivelled.

Plants attacked: Any cuttings as they are rooting or have rooted, but particularly pelargoniums.

Prevention: Use only sterile compost and clean (disinfected) trays and pots. Never use water from water butts for seedlings.

Control: Remove and burn infected plants. When taking cuttings, always use a sharp, clean knife to avoid crushing or bruising the base of the cuttings.

PEONY WILT

A fungus (*Botrytis paeoniae*) invades the base of the stem or top of the root system. It is usually present in the soil but spreads to the plant by water splashes.

Symptoms: The plant's stems and leaves wilt, causing whole shoots to wither and die.

Plants attacked: Mostly herbaceous peonies but tree peonies may also be attacked.

Prevention: There is no fungicide available to amateur gardeners to treat peony wilt.

Control: Cut out infected stems and sections of root to remove any dead or infected tissue. Treat cuts with sulphur dust.

ROSE WILT

The virus (of several species) can be transmitted to healthy plants that have been propagated by budding or grafting or by aphids sucking sap from infected plants.

Symptoms: Growth is stunted, the foliage is mottled with yellow, and there are many small distorted growths, which wilt in warm weather but appear to recover overnight. Plants may just collapse and die.

Plants attacked: Any species or cultivar of rose.

Prevention: There is no possible prevention, apart from purchasing plants only from reputable sources.

Control: There is no control. Remove and burn infected plants as soon as symptoms show.

TOMATO BACTERIAL CANKER

The canker is caused by a soil- and seed-borne bacterium (*Clavibacter michiganensis*), which usually develops as the fruits begin to ripen. It generally enters the plant through injured roots.

Symptoms: The upper leaves wilt suddenly, while the lower leaves turn brown and die. Brown staining is seen on the roots and stems.

Plants attacked: Tomatoes and, possibly, relatives.

Prevention: Do not save seed from infected plants. Disinfect the greenhouse regularly. Employ frequent crop rotation outdoors. Grow plants in growing bags.

Control: Remove and burn infected plants and remove contaminated soil. Apply a dilute solution of cresylic acid to the infected area, which may provide some control.

VERTICILLIUM WILT

The soil-borne fungi (*Verticillium albo-atrum* and *V. dahliae*) are present in the soil in plant debris but are often a serious problem only in heavy or poorly drained soils.

Symptoms: Brown staining occurs in the roots and lower stem. Plants wilt during the day but recover at night. There is a gradual deterioration of overall growth.

Plants attacked: Woody and herbaceous perennials, and vegetables; Japanese maples (*Acer palmatum*) are particularly susceptible.

Prevention: Observe good crop rotation. Use only healthy plants for propagation.

Control: Remove and burn infected plants. Apply a dilute solution of cresylic acid to the infected area, as this may provide some control, although there is no specific fungicide available to amateur gardeners to deal with this fungus.

DID YOU KNOW?

That box blight is caused by a microfungus, *Cylindrocladium*, which is so small that it is almost impossible to detect with the naked eye. Often it is impossible to detect until the host plant is almost dead from the infection.

PLANT PROBLEMS:
the whole plant

Almost everything that attacks a plant has an effect on its overall health and well-being by interfering with its ability to make and use food, and, therefore, to grow, flower and fruit. Some problems will result in the death of the plant if it progresses beyond recovery, where the disruption has weakened the plant to the 'point of no return'. Viruses, for instance, will invade the entire cell system, regardless of how or where they initially entered the plant, even if the visible signs are limited. A problem that attacks the roots may well result in the death of the whole plant if it is not treated in time.

Some problems, however, do literally attack the whole plant at once. Many of these are caused by deficiencies in the medium in which the plant is growing, such as garden soil or compost. You can waste valuable time looking for a pest or injury through which a disease could have entered if you do not take nutrient deficiency into account when you start trying to identify what is affecting the plant. One of the most common, lime-induced chlorosis, occurs if you try to grow acid-loving plants in an alkaline soil. If you invest in a small pH soil-testing kit before you start planting, you can find out whether the plants you are intending to purchase will thrive, survive or die in your soil. If your soil is completely wrong, you can always grow the plants in containers, where you can control the medium more closely by using, say, ericaceous compost if you want to grow

azaleas but have very alkaline soil. A mineral deficiency is relatively easy to correct and can be prevented from happening at all if you establish a regular routine of feeding the plants with a complete fertilizer containing both trace elements and the major nutrients.

Many diseases that affect entire plants have a nasty habit of remaining in the soil for several years after killing the original host, and it is as well to avoid replacing the plant with the same species, at least in the exact spot. Among the best known of these is rose replant disease (one of the specific replant diseases), which is caused by the removal of a large, established plant. A large colony of bacteria and fungi will have built up around the roots or the plant, living with and off the rose and, in turn, breaking down nutrients within the soil for the rose to feed on. The colony grows in relationship to the rose but will completely overwhelm and kill the small root system of a new plant put into the same spot.

A problem such as clematis wilt can appear to kill the whole plant, causing it to turn black and die off, but do not be too hasty in digging it up and throwing it away, because the plant will sometimes recover by producing buds from below ground level.

Other problems, such as blackcurrant reversion, are, however, completely fatal, not treatable, and worst of all, highly contagious. Plants showing these symptoms need to be dug up and burned as quickly as possible.

biting and burrowing pests

ANGLE SHADES MOTH

Females of the insect (*Phlogophora meticulosa*) lay batches of up to 100 eggs on the leaves and stems of plants from late spring until early autumn. The females are green, fawn and pink in colour.

Symptoms: The leaves, buds, flowers and stems are eaten by a greenish-brown caterpillar, with white and grey markings and up to 5cm (2in) long, which feeds at night.

Plants attacked: A wide range of plants, especially houseplants and greenhouse plants, such as chrysanthemums. Also herbaceous plants growing outdoors.

Prevention: Observe good hygiene in greenhouses and conservatories. Remove any loose plant debris.

Control: Spray with bifenthrin or an insecticide based on a plant extract, such as rape seed oil or fatty acids.

ASPARAGUS BEETLE

The insect (*Crioceris asparagi*) can be seen as a 7mm (about ¼in) long black beetle, with yellow spots, or as a creamy-black grub up to 1cm (½in) long.

Symptoms: Plants lose their foliage and stems as adults and larvae eat the leaves and bark from the stems. Stems turn yellow and brown as they die.

Plants attacked: Asparagus, but possibly other members of the Liliaceae family.

Prevention: Burn old stems in autumn and clear up and burn any residual plant debris.

Control: Spray with bifenthrin or an insecticide based on a plant extract, such as rape seed oil or fatty acids.

COLORADO BEETLE

The beetles (*Leptinotarsa decemlineata*) lay up to 500 eggs each and are a serious pest. In Britain any sightings must be reported to the Department for Environment, Food and Rural Affairs (DEFRA).

Symptoms: The leaves, buds, flowers and stems are eaten by yellowish-orange, black-striped adults, up to 1cm (½in) long, and by the similarly sized, bright orange-red, black-spotted larvae.

Plants attacked: Aubergines (eggplants), peppers, tomatoes and potatoes. Other members of the Solanaceae family, such as deadly nightshade (*Atropa belladonna*) and thorn apple (Jimson weed; *Datura stramonium*), may also be attacked.

Prevention: Deep cultivation in autumn will expose the hibernating adults, which can be up to 25cm (10in) deep in the soil.

Control: Spray bifenthrin or an insecticide based on a plant extract, such as rape seed oil or fatty acids, over the host plant.

GOAT MOTH

This pest (*Cossus cossus*) is not common but causes great consternation when it does occur. Often hundreds of caterpillars will feed in one tree for up to four years.

Symptoms: Large caterpillars, to 10cm (4in) long, pink and rusty brown in colour, burrow holes up to 12mm (about ½in) in diameter into the stems of trees, leaving many small heaps of sawdust around the base of the tree. Shoots wilt and die, leaves wither, and the tree becomes structurally unsafe.

Plants attacked: Mature trees, including ash (*Fraxinus*), beech (*Fagus*), elm (*Ulmus*), oak (*Quercus*) and poplar (*Populus*).

Prevention: Spray the stems of trees with insecticide in midsummer to kill adults and eggs.

Control: Spray bifenthrin or an insecticide based on a plant extract, such as rape seed oil or fatty acids, into the holes in the host plant.

RASPBERRY MOTH

The raspberry moth (*Lampronia rubiella*) lays eggs on the flowers. As the eggs hatch, caterpillars feed on the ripening fruits before overwintering and then tunnelling into shoots and buds the following spring.

Symptoms: The young shoots of cane fruits wilt, shrivel and collapse before dying. Pinkish-red caterpillars, about 15mm (¾in) long, are found in cavities in the stems of affected shoots.

Plants attacked: Blackberries, loganberries and raspberries.

Prevention: Reduce numbers of overwintering caterpillars by pruning out old canes. Clear up any leaf litter and plant debris.

Control: Spray canes and soil in midwinter with a tar distillate.

wilts and rots

BEAN ANTHRACNOSE

This fungus, *Colletotrichum lindemuthianum,* is often carried on the seeds and emerges to infect plants as the seed germinates.

Symptoms: Long, narrow, sunken brown marks are seen on the stem. Leaves develop red and brown markings along the veins before they wither and die. Reddish-brown spots appear on leaves and pods. A pinkish, slimy coating of mould may develop over the entire plant.

Plants attacked: Dwarf or runner beans.

Prevention: Grow resistant cultivars, such as 'Aramis' and 'Rido Kenyan'. Use only seed obtained from a reputable seed merchant, do not collect and save seed from infected plants. Avoid growing related crops on the affected site for 5 years if possible.

Control: Remove and burn infected plants.

BEAN CHOCOLATE SPOT

The fungus (*Botrytis fabae*) starts as leaf spots, which spread over the entire plant, causing it to rot and turn black. Even slight attacks greatly reduce crop yields.

Symptoms: Chocolate brown spots are seen on the upper surfaces of the leaves. Streaks appear on flowers, pods and stems. Severely affected plants turn black, wither and die.

Plants attacked: Broad beans.

Prevention: Apply potash to harden growth. Increase the spaces around plants. Improve soil drainage.

Control: Spray with a copper-based fungicide until just before flowering. Remove and burn badly infected plants.

CLEMATIS WILT

This disease, caused by a fungus (*Ascochyta clematidina*), is a common and widespread problem on cultivated clematis.

Symptoms: Young shoots suddenly wilt and collapse, usually when they have been growing rapidly. Dark patches appear on older leaves, and open, discoloured marks are seen on the stems.

Plants attacked: Hybrid clematis, particularly the large, summer-flowering cultivars, which can collapse and die within days.

Prevention: Avoid damaging the base of the stem when weeding. Grow *Clematis viticella* types, which appear to offer some resistance.

Control: Remove and burn infected stems and leaves. Apply cresylic acid as a soil drench around the plant. Some plants may recover and re-grow from the base.

SPECIFIC REPLANT DISEASE

This is not actually a disease but is caused by the high levels of fungi and other micro-organisms that have built up a symbiotic relationship with those plants previously occupying the site.

Symptoms: Plants put on poor, weak growth. New young plants fail to establish and gradually decline, with dieback increasing over a period of three to five years before death.

Plants attacked: Many plants may suffer, but especially members of the Rosaceae family, including apples

(*Malus*), cherries and plums (*Prunus*), pears (*Pyrus*) and roses.

Prevention: Avoid planting the same genus of plant into the same site; for example, do not immediately plant roses back into the site of an old rose bed.

Control: Clean the soil. Treat the planting holes with a mixture of shredded bark and cresylic acid, incorporated according to the manufacturer's recommendations.

STEM AND FRUIT ROT

This disease, which is caused by a fungus (*Didymella lycopersici*), is a common and widespread problem of tomatoes grown under glass or polythene and an even greater problem of those grown outdoors.

Symptoms: Sunken brown lesions are seen on the stem and roots. The lower leaves turn yellow, and fruits become blackened around the calyx as the rot spreads into the flesh. The lesions may girdle the stem at any point and cause the plant to collapse.

Plants attacked: Tomatoes and aubergines (eggplants).

Prevention: Practise good crop hygiene, by sterilizing pots and trays and clearing away old crop debris. Grow plants in growing bags rather than in infected soil.

Control: Remove and burn infected plants. Keep the greenhouse well ventilated.

viruses and bacteria

BACTERIAL CANKER

Caused by a bacterium (*Pseudomonas mors-prunorum*), this disease invades the flowers, leaves, shoots, stems and branches. Mild attacks are often seen as shot-hole symptoms (holes in the leaves).

Symptoms: There are depressed areas of bark with open, watery lesions. Later, branches above the wound die. Leaves and short spurs wilt and turn brown. Blossoms collapse, turn brown and hang on the plant. Wet, open wounds will often spread infection to surrounding plants.

Plants attacked: Fruiting and ornamental plums and cherries (*Prunus*). Other species of *Prunus* are affected by a different kind of bacterial canker.

Prevention: Avoid damaging plants when harvesting and pruning. Improve the drainage. Grow resistant cultivars of plum, such as 'Marjorie's Seedling' or 'Warwickshire Drooper', and of cherry, such as 'Stella' or 'Merton Glory'.

Control: Prune out infected branches. Dig up and burn badly affected plants. Spray with a copper-based fungicide in late summer, early autumn and spring.

BLACKCURRANT REVERSION

This common and widespread disease is possibly the most usual cause of poor cropping of blackcurrants in domestic gardens, and most gardeners are unaware of its presence.

Symptoms: The leaves turn yellow. Plants exhibit reduced vigour, and there is an overall reduction in the number of flowers produced. When it develops, the fruit is of poor quality.

Plants attacked: Blackcurrants (*Ribes nigrum*) and, possibly, other forms of *Ribes*.

Prevention: Avoid plants that show signs of gall mite (big bud; see page 54), because the mites that cause this condition are believed to transmit the virus while feeding. Grow the cultivar 'Foxendown', which is resistant to the mite.

Control: Remove and burn infected plants as soon as the disease is identified.

CARROT MOTLEY DWARF VIRUS

This combination of two viruses (carrot mottle and carrot red leaf) has such a devastating effect on the plants that they can be killed by the infection. Certainly there is no chance of edible roots being produced.

Symptoms: The foliage is stunted and twisted with yellow and pink tinges. Roots fail to develop, and small roots die. Plants may die completely.

Plants attacked: Carrots and parsley.

Prevention: Grow plants under horticultural fleece to prevent aphids from feeding and transmitting the disease.

Control: There is no control. Remove and burn infected plants as soon as the symptoms show.

PRUNE DWARF VIRUS

This particular virus, which is common and widespread throughout northern Europe, causes a decline that totally debilitates the tree. To make matter worse, experts are uncertain about how it actually spreads from plant to plant.

Symptoms: Leaves are small and narrowed, often paler in colour. Shoot growth is severely retarded and stunted, and despite heavy blossom production, few fruit are produced.

Plants attacked: Almost any *Prunus*, but particularly cropping cultivars of plum (*P. domestica*).

Prevention: Purchase plants only from reputable nurseries or garden centres.

Control: Remove and burn infected plants as soon as the symptoms are noticed.

RASPBERRY YELLOW DWARF

This disease is caused by arabis mosaic virus, which is transmitted by the dagger eelworm (*Xiphenema diversicaudatum*), which can survive in a dormant state for many years in the soil.

Symptoms: Plants affected by this disease produce hardly any fruit and those fruit that are produced are of poor quality. Plants are stunted, reaching only about one-third of their potential height. There are yellow spots and pale yellow patches at intervals along the leaves.

Plants attacked: Cultivated and wild raspberries (*Rubus idaeus*).

Prevention: Purchase plants only from reputable nurseries or garden centres.

Control: Remove and burn infected plants as soon as they are noticed.

nutritional disorders

LIME-INDUCED CHLOROSIS

The presence of high levels of free lime in the soil or compost (a high pH) prevents plants from taking up sufficient quantities of nutrients, such as iron.

Symptoms: Growth is stunted, and leaves turn yellow (exhibit chlorosis), starting between the veins. This affects the older leaves first and spreads to the younger ones later.

Plants attacked: Any plant can be affected, but acid-loving plants (calcifuges), such as azaleas, camellias, some heathers, pieris and rhododendrons, will be the first to show symptoms.

Prevention: Maintain the soil pH below 6.5 by adding well-rotted manure regularly and by applying acidic mulches, such as conifer bark.

Control: Apply sequestered iron as a short-term remedy. In the longer term apply flowers of sulphur at the rate of 1kg (2lb) to 10 square metres (yards) of soil.

MAGNESIUM DEFICIENCY

The lack of available magnesium affects plant growth. This is most commonly seen in light, sandy or acid soils, particularly after periods of heavy rain or prolonged watering.

Symptoms: The lower, older leaves turn yellow between the veins and around the margins, while the younger leaves remain green and healthy looking. These older leaves may later show tinges of red, purple and browning.

Plants attacked: Edible and ornamental plants, soft fruit and vegetables; the deficiency is most commonly seen on tomatoes.

Prevention: Try to maintain a soil pH of 6.5–7.0 and try to avoid adding high levels of potash, which lock up magnesium.

Control: Apply Epsom salts at the rate of 200g in 10 litres (8oz in 2½ gallons) of water as a foliar spray.

NITROGEN DEFICIENCY

The lack of available nitrogen affects plant growth and can occur on almost any soil, especially those with a low content of organic matter. This is often worse in the vegetable garden, where crops are harvested, leaving little material to be returned to the soil for recycling.

Symptoms: Pale green leaves eventually turn yellow and pink. The stems are thin and spindly, and growing tips are stunted.

Plants attacked: Trees, shrubs, herbaceous perennials, fruit, vegetables, greenhouse and indoor plants.

Prevention: Dress the soil regularly with well-rotted manure and balanced compound fertilizers.

Control: In emergencies, apply sulphate of ammonia as a quick remedy. For a longer term solution add a high-nitrogen fertilizer, such as nitro-chalk.

PHOSPHATE DEFICIENCY

The lack of available phosphates affects plant growth. Plants are usually only able to extract about one-third of the phosphorus present in a soil.

Symptoms: Plant growth is reduced. Leaves turn a dull green and eventually yellow. The problem may be worse after periods of heavy rainfall, especially on soils with a low pH.

Plants attacked: Any plant can be affected, but plants growing on clay or organic soils are most susceptible. Seedlings are at greatest risk.

Prevention: Dress the soil regularly with well-rotted manure, which produces organic acids, and balanced compound fertilizers.

Control: For a quick response apply superphosphate immediately. Bonemeal is good for slow, long-term release.

DID YOU KNOW?

If you want good growth and leaves on your plants, the best ratio of nitrogen, phosphate and potash is 1:1:1, but if you are growing your plants to produce flowers and fruits then the best ratio tends to be 1:1:2. If the levels of potash in a soil or compost are too high, this will cause an antagonistic effect, resulting in the plants suffering from induced magnesium deficiency.

PLANT PROBLEMS:
seeds and seedlings

Seeds are the perfect package for new plant life. Each one contains the genetic material that will become the plant and nutrients to sustain it until it can begin manufacturing food for itself through new roots and shoots. These nutrients are stored as starches, which are attractive to many creatures and organisms as food for themselves. We eat them in the form of nuts, beans and peas.

Birds, squirrels and small mammals will all dig up and eat seeds sown outdoors, but by sowing extra and netting the crop, you can usually raise enough for your needs. Many of these creatures will also attack developing seeds while they are still on the plant, costing you the crop. Some pests seem to know exactly when the seed is fully ripe before the gardener does.

Insects are more of a problem as they are so much more difficult to spot. They can easily burrow into the developing seeds and destroy them before you realize they are there. The first you will know of their presence will be as you harvest the seeds and each has a hole in it, or you sow the seed and nothing emerges.

Growing from seed and watching new plants emerge is one of the most satisfying parts of gardening, so it is disappointing when something goes wrong and germination is poor or the seedlings emerge but are mis-shapen. Each seed can support its plant until roots and a shoot have formed, but if something has interfered with the seed during its own formation or storage, the seedling is at an immediate disadvantage. The reserve of nutrient might run out before the seedling is self-sufficient, or it can cause cell distortion as the seedling grows. Soil-borne fungi are among the main culprits here, so it is critical that when you are raising seedlings you keep the environment as clean as possible. Use fresh, compost and wash the containers between use, especially if you have lost a previous batch of seedlings to fungal attack, such as damping off (where seedlings fall over and die).

Disorders are more unpredictable than straightforward attacks by pests, but there are fewer of those that attack plants at this stage. Dormancy in seeds can be tricky, but makes germination, when it does occur, all the more satisfying. With hardy shrubs and trees dormancy is often broken by making sure that the seed undergoes conditions similar to those it would experience in nature, such as a cold winter. You can simulate this by mixing the seed with a little moist sand (to prevent it from drying out) in a plastic bag, which can be placed in your refrigerator for up to six weeks. Other seed needs to be soaked before sowing to soften the hard outer casing, and difficult types may have several different types of dormancy, all of which have to be overcome before the seed will germinate. Some need two winters before germinating, so be patient rather than simply throwing it away.

biting and chewing pests

BEAN SEED BEETLE

This insect (*Bruchus rufimanus*), which is only 3mm (⅛in) long, lays its eggs on pods as the seeds are developing. As the eggs hatch, the grubs burrow into the seeds.

Symptoms: There are holes in the seeds, and there is often a pale circular patch on the seed coat while the grub is still inside, indicating that a cavity has been eaten inside the seed.

Plants attacked: Beans (particularly broad beans) and peas of all types.

Prevention: Discard any seeds that show signs of having holes burrowed into them.

Control: There is no effective control, although soaking the seeds before sowing them may force some beetles to emerge.

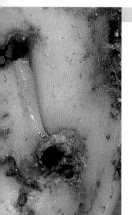

BEAN SEED FLY

The female insect (*Delia platura*) lays eggs in the soil close to the seeds, especially if there is plenty of organic matter present.

Symptoms: Germinating seeds and young seedlings develop ragged leaves and quickly die. Small white maggots, about 8mm (about ¼in) long, feed on the plants, which may recover to produce stunted, distorted growth.

Plants attacked: French and runner beans, and peas.

Prevention: This is more of a problem when germination is slow. Raise plants in pots before transplanting them.

Control: Spray and drench the soil with derris as soon as the damage is seen.

CUTWORM

Soil-dwelling caterpillars, also known as surface caterpillars or brown grubs, of the night-flying large yellow underwing moth (*Noctua pronuba*), are up to 4cm (1½in) long. They are creamy-brown with rows of darker markings along the body.
Symptoms: Small plants and seedlings suddenly wilt and die, with the roots or base of the stem eaten away. This damage usually occurs in succession along the row.
Plants attacked: A wide range of vegetables and ornamental plants, mainly seedlings and young plants.
Prevention: Keep the soil well cultivated and weed free. When damage is found, search in the soil around the dead seedlings; usually the offending cutworm can be found and destroyed.
Control: Drench with derris as soon as the damage is seen. Introduce the pathogenic eelworm *Steinernema carpocapsae* as a biological control.

GREY SQUIRREL

This pest frequents broad-leaved woodland and invades the garden to feed on a range of fruit, vegetables and ornamental plants. They usually produce one or two litters of young each year.
Symptoms: The chewed remains of hazel nuts, pine cones, strawberries, walnuts and a range of berries and fruits will be seen, some as debris on the ground or as partially eaten fruit and seeds on trees and other plants.
Plants attacked: A wide range of plants is attacked, especially in autumn.
Prevention: Prevention is not really possible, as grey squirrels have been known to chew through chicken wire.
Control: Use a bait of seed treated with chilli pepper extract to deter visits into the garden.

NUT WEEVIL

A brown weevil (*Curculio nucum*), about 1cm (½in) long, lays eggs on the leaves or young nuts in midsummer.
Symptoms: Neat round holes, 1–2mm (⅟₁₆in) in diameter, can be seen in maturing cobnut and hazel nut shells where beetle grubs have bored their way out. The nuts are empty, because the small white grub with a brown head has eaten it before leaving the nut.
Plants attacked: Cobnuts and hazel nuts.
Prevention: There is no pesticide available. Gather up and destroy infested nuts.
Control: Spray the developing nuts with derris or pyrethrum to control the adult females and prevent them laying eggs.

wilts and rots

DAMPING OFF

This is caused by a group of soil-borne fungi, including *Phytophthora*, *Pythium* and *Rhizoctonia* spp., which invade and kill the host plants. It is a particular problem with bedding plants and seedlings.

Symptoms: Seedlings fail to emerge after germination, or they fall over, rot and die soon after germination. A furry fungal growth may spread over the dying seedlings and the surrounding compost.

Plants attacked: Young seedlings (usually within five days of germinating); bedding plants and houseplants are often the most vulnerable.

Prevention: Practise good plant care and hygiene. When raising young plants, use sterilized compost and containers. Use seed that has been treated with an appropriate fungicide. Drench seedlings with a copper-based fungicide as soon as they emerge.

Control: Drench infected seedlings and seed trays with a copper-based fungicide.

ERGOT

A fungus (*Claviceps purpurea*) forms on the flowers and seeds of wild and cultivated grasses. Although not common, plants showing symptoms should be handled with care as the fungal spores can cause hallucinations, nausea and convulsions if ingested.

Symptoms: Hard, blackish-purple protrusions are interspersed between the seeds on the seedheads. Seeds are often damaged or destroyed by the disease.

Plants attacked: Many wild grasses, some lawn grasses and some cereals.

Prevention: Mow down and burn any infected seedheads as soon as they are spotted. Wash hands afterwards.

Control: There is no control; see prevention.

TOMATO ASPERMY VIRUS

This virus is common in chrysanthemums and is usually transmitted to other plants by the peach–potato aphid (*Myzus persicae*) as it migrates from one host to another.

Symptoms: Plants produce short, stunted growths and appear as bushes rather than trailing plants. Leaves are distorted and have a pale yellow mottling over the surface. Fruits are small and seedless, or the seed may fail to develop and just rot.

Plants attacked: Tomatoes, peppers and aubergines (eggplants).

Prevention: Avoid growing chrysanthemums and tomatoes close together.

Control: Remove and burn infected plants. If plants do produce seeds, discard them.

BALLING OF ROSES

Balling of roses is a disorder that is caused by the inability of the young blooms to shed water after rain or heavy dew. Grey mould (Botrytis cinerea) will be evident.

Symptoms: Rose buds develop normally, but fail to open, often turning a pale-brown colour, and the flower will collapse and fall apart when touched.

Plants attacked: Roses, particularly hybrid tea roses and old English roses.

Prevention: Grow cultivars that do not have large numbers of petals.

Control: Gently tap the rose bushes after heavy rain or dew to encourage water to drain out from between the petals.

DID YOU KNOW?

Some viruses, such as Cucumber Mosaic Virus, are so mobile that they can be spread from one plant to another just by brushing past them and transmitting the disease on the surface of your clothing.

disorders

BLINDNESS

This disorder can be caused by a range of factors, such as an attack by a pest or disease, drought, waterlogging and even a genetic disturbance within the growing point of the plant.

Symptoms: Extension growth stops because of damage to, or the absence of, a growing point in the tip of the shoot. In the case of oak (*Quercus*), many small shoots emerge just behind the growing point, forming a bird's nest-like rosette.

Plants attacked: A range of plants, including broccoli, cauliflower.

Prevention: Avoid soil or compost that is too wet and maintain a well-balanced nutritional regime.

Control: There is no control; see prevention.

MARSH SPOT

This disorder is caused by manganese deficiency and is particularly common on poor, sandy soils or soils with high levels of organic matter.

Symptoms: The lower, older leaves show yellowing between the veins, while the younger leaves remain green and healthy-looking. Seeds, when split open, show a brown, sunken area in the centre. Affected seeds often fail to germinate or produce stunted, distorted growth.

Plants attacked: Peas and beans.

Prevention: Try to maintain a pH of 6.5–7.0 and improve soil drainage.

Control: Apply manganese sulphate at the rate of 1.5g to 2 square metres (yards) or a balanced, controlled-release fertilizer.

SEED DORMANCY

The seeds of many woody plants fail to germinate because of a chemical or physical barrier within or around the seed Although confusing, this condition can usually be overcome given time.

Symptoms: Seeds fail to germinate, even when the ideal conditions are provided for germination to take place.

Plants attacked: A wide range of plants, but usually much more common in hardy, woody plants, such as trees and shrubs.

Prevention: Harvest the seed just before the fruit is fully ripened to reduce the amount of growth inhibitor present in the seed.

Control: Stratify the seed by placing it in moist sand for a year before sowing.

THERMODORMANCY

This physiological disorder is brought about by sowing seeds in warm compost or soil, which damages the germination and development processes of seeds and seedlings.

Symptoms: Seedlings start to emerge and are checked when growth slows down and stops, often starting again later, but the seedlings are distorted, stunted and may fail to develop fully.

Plants attacked: Many plants, but especially lettuce and members of the Rosaceae family, particularly *Malus* spp.

Prevention: Sow seeds in the evening into cool soil or compost and water immediately; alternatively, sow seeds at dawn to keep soil and compost temperatures low.

Control: Sow Cos (romaine) lettuces, which are less susceptible.

DID YOU KNOW?

The specialised bootlace roots (*rhizomorphs*) of honey fungus (*Armillaria*) can spread through the soil at a rate of 1 metre (3ft) a year in search of a new host to attack.

Key

Part of plant attacked
L = leaves
A = all over the plant
R = root
St = stem
S = seeds or
seedlings
F = flowers or fruits

Time of year
1 = mid winter
2 = late winter
3 = early spring
4 = mid spring
5 = late spring
6 = early summer
7 = mid summer
8 = late summer
9 = early autumn
10 = mid autumn
11 = late autumn
12 = early winter

PROBLEM	PART OF PLANT ATTACKED	TIME OF YEAR	PLANTS ATTACKED
Angle shades moth	A	5–10	A wide range of plants, especially houseplants and greenhouse plants, such as chrysanthemums; also herbaceous plants outdoors
Antirrhinum rust	L	4–9	Antirrhinums
Ant	R	5–8	Many, including fruits, vegetables and ornamental and indoor plants
Azalea gall	St	1–2	Indoor rhododendrons and azaleas as well as outdoor azaleas
Bacterial canker	A	4–9	Fruiting and ornamental plums and cherries (*Prunus* spp.)
Box blight	L	4–9	Box (*Buxus*) spp. and cultivars
Bud blast	F	9–3	Azaleas and rhododendrons
Capsid bug	St	5–6	Many plants, including caryopteris, chrysanthemums, currants (*Ribes*), dahlias, forsythias, fuchsias, hydrangeas and roses
Carnation fly	L	10–12	Carnations, pinks and sweet williams (*Dianthus* spp.)
Carnation wilt	R	4–9	Carnations and pinks (*Dianthus* spp.)
Chafer grub	R	6–8	Lawns, young bedding and ornamental plants, and vegetables
Chrysanthemum white rust	L	1–12	All types of chrysanthemum

PROBLEM	PART OF PLANT ATTACKED	TIME OF YEAR	PLANTS ATTACKED
Clematis wilt	A	4–9	Hybrid clematis, particularly the large, summer-flowering types
Colour-breaking virus	F	1–12	A wide range of plants by a number of different types of viruses and related, virus-like diseases
Coral spot	St	1–12	A wide range of woody plants, including Japanese maples (*Acer palmatum*), magnolias, mulberries (*Morus*), pyracanthas and walnuts (*Juglans*)
Crown gall	St	1–12	Many, including fruit, vegetables and both woody and herbaceous ornamental plants
Dahlia smut	L	7–10	Dahlias of all types
Deer	St	1–12	Almost anything, but less likely to be woody plants, such as roses and shrubs
Dutch elm disease	St	4–9	Many elms (*Ulmus*) and *Zelkova* spp.
Fairy ring	R	6–10	Fine quality turf grasses, especially in intensively managed lawns
Fasciation	St	1–12	Almost any plant can show symptoms, but it is more noticeable on woody subjects
Giant polypore	A	1–12	A wide range of trees, including beech (*Fagus*), birch (*Betula*), oak (*Quercus*) and sweet chestnut (*Castanea sativa*)

Key

Part of plant attacked

L = leaves
A = all over the plant
R = root
St = stem
S = seeds or
seedlings
F = flowers or fruits

Time of year

1 = mid winter
2 = late winter
3 = early spring
4 = mid spring
5 = late spring
6 = early summer
7 = mid summer
8 = late summer
9 = early autumn
10 = mid autumn
11 = late autumn
12 = early winter

PROBLEM	PART OF PLANT ATTACKED	TIME OF YEAR	PLANTS ATTACKED
Greenhouse red spider mite	L	1–12	Many plants will be attacked, but vines, carnations, chrysanthemums, melons and cucumbers are particularly susceptible
Grey squirrel	S	1–12	A wide range of plants is attacked, especially in autumn
Honey fungus	R	4–9	A wide range of plants, including trees, shrubs and herbaceous perennials
Leopard moth	St	4–8	Trees, mainly apple, ash (*Fraxinus*), birch (*Betula*), hawthorn (*Crataegus*), maple (*Acer*), oak (*Quercus*) and pear (*Pyrus*)
Lily beetle	L	5–6	Lily (*Lilium*) spp. and *Fritillaria* spp.
Michaelmas daisy wilt	R	6–9	*Aster* spp. and close relatives
Narcissus fly	St	9–3	Daffodils (*Narcissus* spp.) and many other bulbs
Pansy sickness	R	1–12	Pansies (*Viola* spp.)
Peach leaf curl	L	5–6	Plum, cherries and other members of the genus *Prunus*
Pelargonium blackleg	R	1–12	Any cuttings as they are rooting or have rooted, but particularly pelargoniums
Pelargonium rust	L	1–12	All types of pelargonium apart from ivy-leaved forms

PROBLEM	PART OF PLANT ATTACKED	TIME OF YEAR	PLANTS ATTACKED
Peony wilt	R	5–6	Mostly herbaceous peonies but tree peonies may also be attacked
Petal blight	F	3–5	Cropping and ornamental apples (*Malus* spp.), cherries, (*Prunus* spp.), pears (*Pyrus* spp.) and amelanchiers
Phytophthora root death	R	1–12	Apple (*Malus*), beech (*Fagus*), cherries (*Prunus*), cypress (*Cupressus*), lime (*Tilia*), rhododendron and yew (*Taxus*) and also many ornamental plants
Pineapple gall	St	5–8	Norway spruce (*Picea abies*) and many other species of spruce
Pyracantha scab	F	5–12	Pyracantha
Rabbit	St	1–12	A wide range of trees, mainly young ones and particularly apple (*Malus domestica*) and its relatives
Red thread	L	7–9	Turf, especially certain types of grass including red fescues, bents and meadow grasses
Rhododendron leaf spot	L	1–12	Rhododendrons
Root eelworms	R	1–12	Many vegetables (brassicas, carrots, onions, peas, potatoes, tomatoes), figs and ornamental plants
Rose blackspot	L	4–9	This disease is specific to roses of all kinds

Key

Part of plant attacked

L = leaves
A = all over the plant
R = root
St = stem
S = seeds or
seedlings
F = flowers or fruits

Time of year

1 = mid winter
2 = late winter
3 = early spring
4 = mid spring
5 = late spring
6 = early summer
7 = mid summer
8 = late summer
9 = early autumn
10 = mid autumn
11 = late autumn
12 = early winter

PROBLEM	PART OF PLANT ATTACKED	TIME OF YEAR	PLANTS ATTACKED
Rose gall wasp	St	5–9	Wild and cultivated roses of all types
Rose powdery mildew	L	3–10	This disease is specific to roses of all kinds
Rose rust	L	4–9	This rust is specific to roses
Rose wilt	R	3–10	Any type or species of rose
Sclerotinia disease	R	5–12	A wide range, including herbaceous perennials, chrysanthemums, dahlias and many vegetables
Seed dormancy	S	1–12	A wide range of plants, especially woody trees and shrubs
Slugs	St	3–10	A wide range of plants, including hostas, herbaceous perennials, seedlings and food crops, on any part of the plant they can reach
Small ermine moth	L	4–6	Apple (*Malus*), hawthorn (*Crataegus*), cherry, willow (*Salix*) and many others
Solomon's seal sawfly	L	5–6	Any type of *Polygonatum*
Sparrow	F	1–12	A wide range of plants, including bulbs and soft fruit
Stem and bulb eelworm	St	4–9	A wide range of young plants but particularly phlox and narcissus bulbs, garlic, onions and strawberries
Thrips	St	3–7	A wide range of young plants

PROBLEM	PART OF PLANT ATTACKED	TIME OF YEAR	PLANTS ATTACKED
Vapourer moth	L	5–8	Roses and ornamental trees and shrubs
Verticillium wilt	R	4–9	Woody and herbaceous perennials, and vegetables. Japanese maples (*Acer palmatum*) are particularly susceptible
Viburnum beetle	L	6–8	*Viburnum lantana, V. opulus* and *V. tinus*
Vine weevil	R	9–4	A wide range of plants, including begonias, camellias, cyclamen, fuchsias, primulas and rhododendrons
Waterlily beetle	L	6–8	Waterlilies (*Nymphaea* spp.) only
White root rot	R	1–12	A wide range, including grape vine (*Vitis*), apple (*Malus*), pears (*Pyrus*), potato, flower bulbs and privet (*Ligustrum*)
Wirestem	S	3–8	A wide range of plants, mostly vegetables, and particularly seedlings
Witches' broom	St	1–12	Acacia, birch (*Betula*), cherry and plum (*Prunus*) and hornbeam (*Carpinus*) are regularly affected but other plants may also carry them
Woodlice	R	3–10	A wide range of plants, but mainly seedlings of vegetables and bedding plants and young vegetables

Key

Part of plant attacked

L = leaves
A = all over the plant
R = root
St = stem
S = seeds or
seedlings
F = flowers or fruits

Time of year

1 = mid winter
2 = late winter
3 = early spring
4 = mid spring
5 = late spring
6 = early summer
7 = mid summer
8 = late summer
9 = early autumn
10 = mid autumn
11 = late autumn
12 = early winter

PROBLEM	PART OF PLANT ATTACKED	TIME OF YEAR	PLANTS ATTACKED
Apple blossom weevil	F	3–5	Cropping and ornamental apples (*Malus*), both spp and cvs.
Apple canker	St	1–12	A wide range of plants, including apple (*Malus*), beech (*Fagus*), hawthorn (*Crataegus*), pear (*Pyrus*), poplar (*Populus*), *Sorbus* and willow (*Salix*)
Apple powdery mildew	L	3–10	Cropping and ornamental apples (*Malus*), medlars (*Mespilus*), pears (*Pyrus*) and quince (*Cydonia*)
Apple sawfly	F	6–7	Most dessert apples (*Malus*); cooking apples are rarely attacked
Apple scab	L	4–9	Cropping and ornamental apples (*Malus*), particularly in wet years
Bitter pit	F	9–10	Apples (*Malus*)
Blackcurrant gall mite	L	3–5	Blackcurrants, although related species of the mite attack hazel (*Corylus*) and yew (*Taxus*)
Blackcurrant reversion	A	1–12	Blackcurrants and possibly other forms of *Ribes*
Brown rot	F	7–10	Apples (*Malus*), nectarines, peaches and plums (*Prunus*) and pears (*Pyrus*)
Bullfinch	F	11–3	Many, including apple, cherry and plum, forsythia, gooseberry and pears (*Pyrus*)

PROBLEM	PART OF PLANT ATTACKED	TIME OF YEAR	PLANTS ATTACKED
Capsid bug	F	5–6	A wide range, including apples (*Malus*), currants, gooseberries, raspberries and strawberries, as well as many ornamental plants
Codling moth	F	6–7	Apples (*Malus*) and occasionally pears (*Pyrus*), medlars (*Mespilus*) and quinces (*Cydonia*)
Fireblight	St	4–6	Many members of the rose family: cotoneasters, crab apple (*Malus*), hawthorn (*Crataegus*), pyracanthas, *Sorbus* and quince (*Cydonia*)
Goat moth	A	4–8	Mature trees: ash (*Fraxinus*), beech (*Fagus*), elm (*Ulmus*), oak (*Quercus*) and poplar (*Populus*).
Gooseberry sawfly	L	5–6	Gooseberry, redcurrant and white currant
Nut weevil	S	7–8	Cobnuts and hazel nuts
Peach–potato aphid	St	4–10	A wide range of plants, including trees, shrubs, climbers, all vegetable and fruit crops
Pear midge	F	4–5	Fruiting and ornamental pears (*Pyrus*)
Plum moth	F	6–8	Damsons, greengages and plums (*Prunus*)
Prune dwarf virus	A	4–10	Almost any member of *Prunus* genus, but particularly cropping cvs. of plum

Key

Part of plant attacked
L = leaves
A = all over the plant
R = root
St = stem
S = seeds or
seedlings
F = flowers or fruits

Time of year
1 = mid winter
2 = late winter
3 = early spring
4 = mid spring
5 = late spring
6 = early summer
7 = mid summer
8 = late summer
9 = early autumn
10 = mid autumn
11 = late autumn
12 = early winter

PROBLEM	PART OF PLANT ATTACKED	TIME OF YEAR	PLANTS ATTACKED
Raspberry moth	A	4–6	Blackberries, loganberries and raspberries
Raspberry yellow dwarf	A	4–10	Cultivated and wild raspberries
Silver leaf	St	4–10	Any relative of the cherry (*Prunus*), both ornamental and fruiting, that has just been pruned may become infected and killed; poplars (*Populus*) may also be attacked
Slugworm	L	4–10	Pears, cherries and plums, hawthorn (*Crataegus*), *Sorbus* and quince (*Cydonia*)
Specific replant disease	A	1–12	Many plants may suffer, especially members of the rose family, including apples (*Malus*), cherries and plums (*Prunus*), pears (*Pyrus*) and roses
Stony pit	F	9–11	Pears (*Pyrus*) and quince (*Cydonia*)
Strawberry red core	R	4–10	Strawberries (*Fragaria* spp.)
Tarsonemid mite	L	4–10	Mainly plants growing in greenhouses, houses and conservatories
Walnut soft shell rot	S	1–12	Most types of walnut (*Juglans*)
Wasps	F	7–10	Any fruits, particularly plums and apples
Winter moth	F	4–6	Most cropping fruit trees and many ornamental plants

PROBLEM	PART OF PLANT ATTACKED	TIME OF YEAR	PLANTS ATTACKED
Asparagus beetle	A	4–9	Asparagus, but perhaps other members of the lily family
Bean anthracnose	A	5–8	Dwarf or runner beans
Bean chocolate spot	A	3–10	Broad beans
Bean seed beetle	St	7–9	Beans (particularly broad beans) and peas of all types
Bean seed fly	S	4–6	French and runner beans, as well as peas
Black bean aphid	St	4–10	A wide range of fruit, vegetables and ornamental plants
Blindness	S	4–7	A range of plants, including broccoli, cauliflower and many other seedlings
Blossom end rot	F	5–10	Tomatoes and peppers
Brassica downy mildew	L	4–10	Any member of the brassica family, related weeds and ornamental plants, such as alyssum and wallflowers (*Erysimum*)
Cabbage root fly	R	4–9	Any member of the brassica family as well as ornamental plants, such as alyssum, aubrietas, stocks (*Matthiola*) and wallflowers (*Erysimum*)
Cabbage white	L	4–9	All brassicas and nasturtiums (*Tropaeolum*)
Carrot motley dwarf virus	A	1–12	Carrots and parsley

Key

Part of plant attacked
L = leaves
A = all over the plant
R = root
St = stem
S = seeds or
seedlings
F = flowers or fruits

Time of year
1 = mid winter
2 = late winter
3 = early spring
4 = mid spring
5 = late spring
6 = early summer
7 = mid summer
8 = late summer
9 = early autumn
10 = mid autumn
11 = late autumn
12 = early winter

PROBLEM	PART OF PLANT ATTACKED	TIME OF YEAR	PLANTS ATTACKED
Carrot root fly	R	4–9	Celery, celeriac, carrots, fennel, parsley and parsnips
Clubroot root	R	1–12	This disease will attack all members of the cabbage family (brassicas) and its relatives
Colorado beetle	A	5–7	Aubergines (eggplants), peppers, potatoes and tomatoes
Cutworm	R	6–9	Many, but particularly young vegetable plants, and strawberries, chrysanthemums and dahlias
Flea beetle	L	4–10	Radish, swede and turnip; also alyssum, aubrieta, nasturtiums (*Tropaeolum*), stocks (*Matthiola*) and wallflowers (*Erysimum*)
Leatherjackets	R	9–5	Young vegetables and salad crops, and many ornamental plants, including turf
Marsh spot	S	6–10	Peas and beans
Mealy cabbage aphid	L	6–9	All members of the cabbage family, particularly the leafy vegetables
Onion fly	R	5–7	Chives, garlic, leeks, shallots and salad onions
Onion white rot	R	1–12	Chives, garlic, leeks, shallots and salad onions
Pea moth	F	7–8	Peas of many types

PROBLEM	PART OF PLANT ATTACKED	TIME OF YEAR	PLANTS ATTACKED
Pea wilt	R	5–9	Peas and close relatives, including sweet peas (*Lathyrus*)
Potato blackleg	R	5–8	Potatoes, and possibly weeds belonging to the potato family – e.g., black nightshade (*Solanum nigrum*)
Potato blight	L	5–8	Potatoes and tomatoes
Root aphids	R	4–10	French and runner beans, Jerusalem artichokes and lettuce; also auriculas and roses
Root knot eelworms	R	1–12	Carrots, onions, potatoes and tomatoes; also chrysanthemums and cyclamen
Stem and fruit rot	A	4–10	Tomatoes and aubergines (eggplants)
Sweetcorn smut	F	7–9	Sweetcorn, ornamental maize and forage maize
Thermodormancy	S	5–9	Many plants; lettuce and members of the rose family (particularly *Malus*) may also suffer
Tomato aspermy virus	S	1–12	Tomatoes, peppers and aubergines (eggplants)
Tomato bacterial canker	A	5–8	Tomatoes
Violet root rot	A	4–10	Asparagus, beetroot, carrots, celery, parsnips, potatoes, swedes and turnips; also many herbaceous perennials

Key

Part of plant attacked
L = leaves
A = all over the plant
R = root
St = stem
S = seeds or
seedlings
F = flowers or fruits

Time of year
1 = mid winter
2 = late winter
3 = early spring
4 = mid spring
5 = late spring
6 = early summer
7 = mid summer
8 = late summer
9 = early autumn
10 = mid autumn
11 = late autumn
12 = early winter

PROBLEM	PART OF PLANT ATTACKED	TIME OF YEAR	PLANTS ATTACKED
Brown scale	St	1–12	Many ornamental plants, as well as conservatory and greenhouse plants
Chrysanthemum leaf miner	L	1–12	Chrysanthemums; cinerarias (*Pericallis*), gerberas and pyrethrums (*Tanacetum*) are among the many relatives of the chrysanthemum attacked by this pest
Damping off	S	1–12	Young seedlings (usually within 5 days of germinating); bedding plants and houseplants are often the most vulnerable
Earwig	F	5–10	Herbacous perennials, especially chrysanthemums and dahlias, houseplants and young vegetables
Greenhouse thrips	L	1–12	Mainly plants growing in greenhouses, houses and conservatories, but outdoor plants may be attacked
Grey mould	A	1–12	Almost any plant, but particularly soft tissue, such as flower petals and fruits
Mealybug	St	1–12	Many ornamental plants, as well as conservatory and greenhouse plants
Root aphid	R	1–12	Mainly plants growing in greenhouses, houses and conservatories, but outdoor plants may be attacked

PROBLEM	PART OF PLANT ATTACKED	TIME OF YEAR	PLANTS ATTACKED
Root mealybug	R	1–12	Mostly pot plants, such as African violets (*Saintpaulia*), cacti, fuchsias and pelargoniums
Sciarid fly (fungus gnat)	R	1–12	A wide range of indoor tender plants, bedding plants and cuttings
Soft scale	L	1–12	Bay (*Laurus nobilis*), *Citrus*, ivy (*Hedera*), *Ficus* and many conservatory and greenhouse plants
Sun damage	L	5–9	Most plants exposed to hot, bright conditions
Symphylid	R	1–12	A wide range of plants, including bulbs, bedding plants, vegetables and seedlings
Vine weevil	R	9–4	A wide range of plants, including begonias, cyclamen, fuchsias and primulas
Whitefly	L	1–12	A wide range of greenhouse and houseplants, plus outdoor plants in summer
Waterlogging	A	1–12	Any plant

troubleshooting

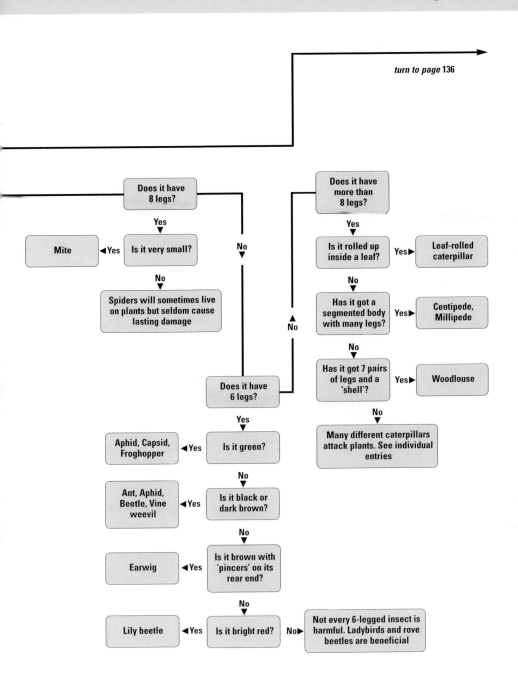

turn to page 136

Does it have 8 legs?

Yes ▼

Is it very small? ◄Yes **Mite**

No ▼

Spiders will sometimes live on plants but seldom cause lasting damage

No ▼

Does it have 6 legs?

Yes ▼

Is it green? ◄Yes **Aphid, Capsid, Froghopper**

No ▼

Is it black or dark brown? ◄Yes **Ant, Aphid, Beetle, Vine weevil**

No ▼

Is it brown with 'pincers' on its rear end? ◄Yes **Earwig**

No ▼

Is it bright red? ◄Yes **Lily beetle**

No ▲

Does it have more than 8 legs?

Yes ▼

Is it rolled up inside a leaf? Yes► **Leaf-rolled caterpillar**

No ▼

Has it got a segmented body with many legs? Yes► **Centipede, Millipede**

No ▼

Has it got 7 pairs of legs and a 'shell'? Yes► **Woodlouse**

No ▼

Many different caterpillars attack plants. See individual entries

No► Not every 6-legged insect is harmful. Ladybirds and rove beetles are beneficial

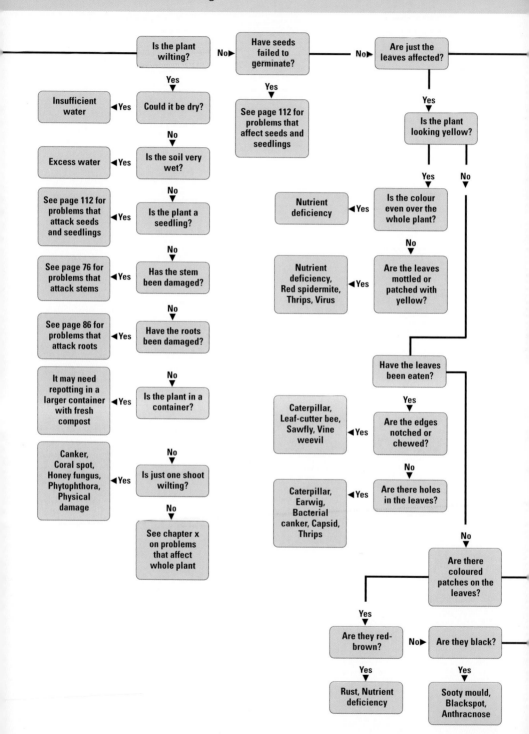

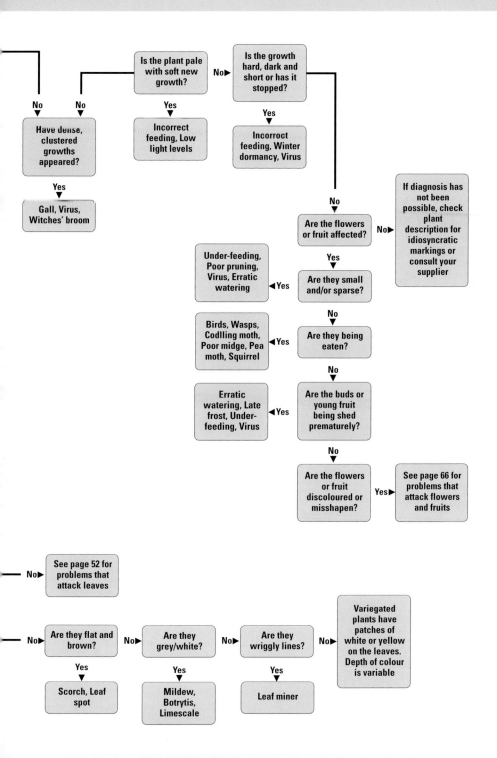

No → **No**

Is the plant pale with soft new growth?

No ▶ Is the growth hard, dark and short or has it stopped?

No ▼ Have dense, clustered growths appeared?

Yes ▼ Incorrect feeding, Low light levels

Yes ▼ Incorrect feeding, Winter dormancy, Virus

Yes ▼ Gall, Virus, Witches' broom

If diagnosis has not been possible, check plant description for idiosyncratic markings or consult your supplier

No ▼ Are the flowers or fruit affected? **No** ▶

Yes ▼

Under-feeding, Poor pruning, Virus, Erratic watering ◀ **Yes** Are they small and/or sparse?

No ▼

Birds, Wasps, Codlling moth, Poor midge, Pea moth, Squirrel ◀ **Yes** Are they being eaten?

No ▼

Erratic watering, Late frost, Under-feeding, Virus ◀ **Yes** Are the buds or young fruit being shed prematurely?

No ▼

Are the flowers or fruit discoloured or misshapen? **Yes** ▶ See page 66 for problems that attack flowers and fruits

No ▶ See page 52 for problems that attack leaves

No ▶ Are they flat and brown? **No** ▶ Are they grey/white? **No** ▶ Are they wriggly lines? **No** ▶ Variegated plants have patches of white or yellow on the leaves. Depth of colour is variable

Yes ▼ Scorch, Leaf spot

Yes ▼ Mildew, Botrytis, Limescale

Yes ▼ Leaf miner

glossary

Abdomen The lower part of an insect's body.

Acaracide A pesticide used to control mites.

Acid Soil that has a pH value of less than 7.0. See also ALKALINE and NEUTRAL.

Alkaline Soil that has a pH value greater than 7.0. See also ACID and NEUTRAL.

Alternate host One of two host plants needed by a pest or disease to complete its lifecycle.

Anaerobe An organism that can live without air or that requires oxygen-free conditions. An anaerobic process can take place in the absence of oxygen.

Annual A fungus or plant that completes its lifecycle, from germination to death, in one year. See also BIENNIAL, PERENNIAL.

Antenna (pl. antennae) A jointed sensory organ on the head of insects and mites.

Anther The part of a stamen that produces pollen.

Anthracnose A fungal disease of plants, seen as dark spots or lesions on foliage, stems, pods or fruits. There are several types, each specific to particular plant groups, such as beans, peas and different tree species (including *Salix* and *Platanus*).

Arthropod A creature with a segmented body and jointed legs – e.g., insects, mites, woodlice, centipedes and millipedes.

Asexual reproduction A form of reproduction that does not involve fertilization. Vine weevils and certain generations of aphid reproduce asexually.

Axil The upper angle between a stem and the leaf that develops from it. The point where an axillary bud develops.

Bacterium (pl. bacteria) A single-celled micro-organism. Many bacteria are beneficial to plants, but others may be pathogenic or cause rotting.

Bactericide A chemical capable of destroying bacteria.

Bark The protective layer of cells on the outer surface of the trunk, branches and stems of trees and woody plants.

Basal plate The compressed stem of a BULB.

Base dressing An application of fertilizer or organic matter that is incorporated into the soil before planting or sowing.

Biennial A plant that completes its lifecycle in two growing seasons, germinating and producing roots and leaves in the first year, and flowering and producing seed before dying in the second year – e.g., common foxglove (*Digitalis purpurea*) and forget-me-not (*Myosotis sylvatica*). See also ANNUAL, PERENNIAL.

Biological control The control of pests, diseases and weeds by the use of natural enemies, such as predators, parasites and pathogens.

Bio-pesticide A parasite predator, bacterium, fungus or virus-like structure used to control pests and diseases.

Bleeding The oozing of sap from a wound or cut.

Blight A type of fungus that attacks certain types of plant..

Blind shoot A shoot that does not form a terminal bud or growing point.

Bolting The premature production of flowers and seeds.

Bordeaux mixture A fungicidal compound containing copper sulphate and quicklime or hydrated lime, which is used to prevent the spread of diseases, including potato blight. It is harmful to some plants and toxic to fish, so use only according to the manufacturer's instructions.

Broad spectrum A chemical that has an effect on a wide range of often unrelated organisms.

Bud A condensed shoot containing embryonic leaves or flowers.

Bud union The point at which a SCION is budded on to a ROOTSTOCK.

Budding A propagation technique, used for roses and fruit trees, by which two (or more) plants are joined together.

Bulb A storage organ, usually but not always found underground, consisting mainly of fleshy scales and swollen, modified leaf bases on a much reduced stem. See also CORM, RHIZOME.

Calcicole A plant that prefers alkaline soil (with a pH greater than 7.0), usually a limey soil.

Calcifuge A plant that prefers acidic soil (with a pH of less than 7.0), usually a peaty or organic soil.

Callus Corky wound tissue produced around the edges of a wound by a plant in response to wounding.

Caterpillar The larval stage of a moth or butterfly.

Chemical A fungicide, pesticide, weedkiller, repellent or fertilizer used to kill or control diseases, pests or weeds or to increase the nutritional value of the soil.

Cheshunt compound A mixture of ammonium carbonate and copper sulphate, used to protect seedlings from fungal attack, including damping off. Toxic to fish.

Chilling A period of low temperature, usually 2.2°C (36°F), required by plants during dormancy to stimulate flower development.

Chlorosis The yellowing of leaf tissue due to a deficiency or loss of chlorophyll (the green pigment). It may be caused by physiological disorders, nutrient deficiencies or pests and diseases.

Chlorotic Showing the symptoms of CHLOROSIS.

Chrysalis The resting, inactive stage of a moth or butterfly between a fully fed caterpillar and the adult insect; also called a PUPA.

Colour-breaking A term used to describe a patterned change in flower colour, where the original colour becomes mixed into elaborate feathered patterns. Parrot and Rembrandt tulips are particularly susceptible.

Companion planting Positioning plants together that have a beneficial effect on neighbouring plants by discouraging pests and diseases.

Complete metamorphosis See METAMORPHOSIS.

Compost (1) A potting medium that consists of a mixture of loam, sand, peat (or peat substitute), leaf mould or other ingredients. (2) An organic material, formed from the decomposed plant remains and other organic matter.

Contact A chemical that remains on the outside of a plant and is absorbed by a pest or disease when it comes into contact with a treated surface. See also SYSTEMIC.

Corm The swollen, usually underground, base of a stem. See also BULB, RHIZOME.

Cotyledon A seed or primary leaf; the first leaf or leaves to emerge after seed germination.

Cruciferous Of the family Cruciferae (also known as Brassicaceae), to which brassicas, alyssum and stocks (*Matthiola*) belong.

Cultivar A plant that has been developed in cultivation rather than occurring naturally in the wild. See also VARIETY.

Deciduous A plant that sheds its leaves or dies down at the end of the growing season (in autumn and winter) and renews them or re-grows at the beginning of the next season.

Defoliation Loss of leaves.

Derris An insecticide derived from the roots of *Derris* and *Lonchocarpus* spp. The active ingredient is rotenone.

Dieback The death of shoots, often spreading down from the tip of the stem.

Dormancy The state of temporary cessation of growth in plants in winter. See also SEED DORMANCY.

Drench A pest or disease control applied as a liquid to the soil around a plant rather than to the leaves.

Drupe See STONE FRUIT.

Dust A pest or disease control applied as a fine dust to the plant or to the soil.

Ectoparasite A parasite that feeds on the outside of a plant – e.g., an aphid.

Eelworm See NEMATODE.

Endoparasite A parasite that feeds inside a plant – e.g., a leaf miner.

Family A category in plant classification, grouping together related genera, all of which have characteristics that are constant. See also GENUS, SPECIES.

Fertilization The fusion of a pollen grain nucleus (male) with an ovule (female) to form a fertile seed.

Frass (1) The excrement of insect larvae. (2) The refuse left by insects, especially wood-boring caterpillars.

Free-living An organism, such as a nematode, that is associated with a host but is not attached to it.

Fruiting body The spore-bearing structure of a fungus.

Fungicide A pesticide capable of controlling a fungus.

Fungus (pl. fungi) A large variable group of organisms, lacking chlorophyll, which obtain their food materials from living on dead or live organic matter.

Gall An abnormal growth produced by a plant in response to chemicals from an insect, fungus or bacterium living within or close to the galled tissue.

Genus (pl. genera) Species that have a large number of features in common are grouped into a genus. See also FAMILY, SPECIES.

Grafting A propagation method involving the joining of two or more separate plants. See also ROOTSTOCK, SCION.

Graft union The point at which a SCION is grafted on to a ROOTSTOCK.

Herbicide A chemical used to kill or control weeds.

Herbivore A plant-feeding animal.

Hermaphrodite A creature with both female and male sexual organs – e.g., slugs, snails and earthworms. Some plants have both male and female organs (pistils and stamens) and do not need a separate pollinator (unless the plant is self-sterile).

Honeydew A sugary liquid excreted by sap-feeding insects, including many, but not all, aphids, whiteflies, suckers, mealybugs and scale insects.

Horticultural fleece A synthetic material composed of fine fibres woven or compressed together into a fabric that can be draped over plants as a barrier to protect them from certain pests or from cold weather.

Host (1) The plant on which an insect, pest or disease feeds and develops. (2) The organism on which a parasite or predator feeds and develops.

Host range The range of host plants on which a given pest or a disease can feed and develop.

Hyphae The thread-like growths formed by a fungus.

Immune A plant with characteristics that prevent a specific pest or pathogen from attacking or colonizing it.

Incomplete metamorphosis See METAMORPHOSIS.

Inorganic Generally, not of plant or animal origin (containing no carbon) – i.e., a mineral or synthetically produced material.

Insect An invertebrate animal whose body is divided into a head, thorax and abdomen. Adult insects have three pairs of jointed legs on the thorax and, usually, two pairs of wings – e.g., moths, butterflies, beetles, ants, bees, wasps, sawflies, some aphids, whitefly and earwigs.

Insecticidal soap A pesticide containing fatty acids that is used to combat some pests, diseases and weeds.

Insecticide A chemical, in the form of a liquid, powder or smoke, that is capable of controlling or killing insects.

Integrated Pest Management (IPM) A combination of cultural, chemical and biological control techniques, aimed at keeping pests and diseases below the level at which damage occurs.

Invertebrate An animal without a backbone - e.g., insects, mites, woodlice, molluscs, nematodes, earthworms and millipedes.

Larva (pl. larvae) The immature feeding-stage in the lifecycle of an insect – e.g., a caterpillar of a moth or butterfly, a grub of a beetle and a maggot of a fly.

Latent infection Infection by a pathogen that does not result in any visible symptoms on the plant – e.g., some viruses.

Leaching Loss of nutrients that are washed down through the soil to areas beyond the reach of a plant's roots.

Lesion A wound or area of damage caused by a pest, disease or physical injury.

Lime A chemical compound of calcium; the amount of lime in soil determines whether it is ALKALINE, NEUTRAL or ACID.

Mandible The upper or lower biting mouthpart of an insect, especially wood- and leaf-eating species.

Metamorphosis The transformation undergone during the development of an organism, such as an insect or mite, from the immature to adult form. Incomplete metamorphosis, as exhibited by aphids, capsid bugs, earwigs and mites, involves little more than an increase in size and the gradual development of sexual organs and, sometimes, wings. Complete metamorphosis involves a dramatic change of form, with the larva bearing no resemblance to the adult, as in moths, flies, beetles and sawflies.

Molluscicide A chemical capable of killing or controlling slugs and snails.

Mutation A plant change or variation that occurs by chance, often referred to as a 'sport'.

Mycelium A network of vegetative HYPHAE from which a FRUITING BODY arises.

Mycoplasma A microscopic parasitic organism, closely related to a virus and with similar characteristics.

Mycorrhiza Beneficial soil fungi that live in mutual association (symbiosis) with plant roots, helping them to absorb nutrients from the soil.

Necrosis The deterioration and death of plant tissue.

Necrotic Dead areas of plant tissue, frequently brown or black.

Nematicide A chemical capable of controlling or killing nematodes (eelworms).

Nematode A microscopic, worm-like creature, also known as an eelworm. Some nematodes are used as pest predators – e.g., the nematode *Phasmarhabditis hermaphrodita* can be used to control slugs.

Neutral Soil with a pH value of 7, the point at which it is neither ACID nor ALKALINE.

Nitrate A salt of nitric acid, having a high nitrogen content that is available to plants, which is either produced by the activity of bacteria in the soil or is manufactured.

Nitrite A salt of nitric acid in which the nitrogen is not readily available to plants.

Node The point on a stem from which one or more buds, leaves, shoots or flowers develop.

Nutrient A mineral (mineral ion) used to develop proteins and other compounds required for plant growth.

Nymph The immature stage of some insects or mites, including aphids and leafhoppers.

Organic (1) Of garden chemicals, referring to compounds containing carbon derived from plant or animal organisms. (2) Mulches, composts or similar materials derived from plant or animal waste. (3) A method of growing and gardening without using synthetic or inorganic materials.

Ovicide A chemical capable of controlling or killing the egg stage of pests.

Ovipositor The egg-laying organ of an insect.

Parasite An organism that obtains all or part of its food from another plant or animal over a period of time, usually without killing its host.

Parthenogenesis The ability of some female pests to reproduce without fertilization. Many aphids have this ability, as have vine weevils, some sawflies and mealybugs. Males are rare or non-existent in these species.

Pathogen A living organism that causes disease in another organism. Pathogens include certain bacteria, fungi, viruses and MYCOPLASMAS.

Pedicel The stalk of an individual flower.

Perennial A plant that lives for two or more years; the word usually refers to an herbaceous perennial. See also ANNUAL, BIENNIAL.

Persistence The length of time a chemical remains in an active form, either on the plant or in the soil or compost after it has been applied.

Pesticide A term usually applied to chemicals that control or kill pests but that is sometimes (wrongly) extended to include fungicides, herbicides and animal repellents.

pH The scale by which the acidity or alkalinity of a soil is measured.

Pheromone A volatile chemical produced by insects as a means of communicating with others of the same species. Males often locate females by tracking down the source of the pheromone or scent released by the female. Pheromone traps are available to trap the males of some moths, including the tortrix moth (*Cacoecimorpha pronubana*) and plum moth (*Cydia funebrana*).

Phloem The conducting tissues within a plant, largely associated with the transportation of food materials in solution, produced in the leaves and distributed to the rest of the plant.

Phytotoxic A chemical (usually a pesticide) that can damage the plant on which it has been sprayed.

Polyphagous A pest that feeds on a wide range of plants, which may be botanically unrelated.

Proboscis An insect's mouthparts, used for sucking liquids, especially nectar, from plants.

Proleg The fleshy leg on the abdomen of a caterpillar or sawfly larva.

Pupa The resting, non-feeding stage in the lifecycle of certain insects; also known as a CHRYSALIS.

Pupation The period during which a larva changes into the form of the adult insect.

Repellent A substance that deters a pest without causing it harm.

Resistant A plant that might be attacked by a pest or disease but shows no ill-effects. A fungus may also develop resistance to a fungicide or to a closely related group of fungicides. Fungicide resistance occurs most commonly when a particular fungicide has been used repeatedly for many years. Similar resistance problems also occur with some pests and weeds that are no longer controlled by insecticides and herbicides that were once effective.

Rhizome A specialized horizontal stem, usually creeping, swollen or slender and growing underground, that acts as a storage organ and produces aerial shoots at its apex and along its length. See also BULB, CORM.

Rhizomorph A cord-like fungal structure that is resilient and withstands extremes of temperature and moisture. Honey fungus rhizomorphs are dark and tough and grow from host to host.

Root The part of a plant, usually underground, that anchors it and through which water and nutrients are absorbed.

Rootstock The lower part of a trunk and its root system on to which another plant, the SCION, is grafted.

Russeting A discoloration, generally brown, on a plant surface (usually the skin of fruits), which is often roughened.

Saprophyte A plant, often a fungus, that lives on dead or decaying organic material but does not attack living material.

Scion The shoot, bud or cutting that is grafted on to another ROOTSTOCK.

Seed dormancy The failure of a seed to germinate when it is placed in conditions suitable for germination. See also DORMANCY.

Shoot The aerial part of a plant that bears leaves. A sideshoot arises from a bud along the length of a main shoot.

Species In plant classification a group of closely related plants that are distinct from others within the same GENUS. A species will consistently come true to type from seed. See also FAMILY.

Spore The microscopic reproductive structure of fungi and bacteria.

Sport See MUTATION.

Spur A short flower- or fruit-bearing branch.

Stem The main axis of a plant, usually above ground and supporting leaves, flowers and fruits.

Stolon A horizontally spreading or branching stem, usually above ground, which roots at its tip to produce a new plant, as with strawberries (*Fragaria* spp.).

Stone fruit A fruit, also known as a drupe, of which the seed (stone) is held within a layer of soft flesh. Many members of the *Prunus* genus – e.g., apricots, cherries, damsons and plums – are simple drupes; raspberries are compound drupes.

Stratification The exposure of seed to conditions (usually cold) that enable it to overcome dormancy.

Stylet The mouthpart of a sap-feeding insect or mite, used for piercing plant tissue.

Systemic A pesticide or fungicide that flows within a plant's sap and is translocated (transported) within the plant. See also CONTACT.

Tender A plant that is killed or damaged by temperatures below –10°C (15°F).

Thorax The mid-part of an insect's body, between the head and abdomen.

Tolerant Able to withstand an attack by a pest or disease.

Transpiration The loss of water through evaporation from the leaves and stems of a plant.

Tuber A swollen, usually underground, organ, derived from a stem or root, that is used for food storage.

Variegated Irregularly marked with various colours, especially leaves, but also petals, that are patterned with markings in white, yellow or other colours.

Variety A plant that has developed with a slight difference from a wild plant SPECIES. Plant varieties are often brought into cultivation once developed. See also CULTIVAR.

Virus A microscopic organism that infects a host and multiplies within the living cells.

Virus vector An insect, mite or nematode that transmits a plant virus, usually on its mouthparts or in its saliva.

Wetting agent A material, such as saponin or soft soap, used to lower the surface tension of liquids on a plant's surface, allowing a spray to form a film over the surface rather than forming into droplets. Many garden pesticide formulations contain wetting agents, which are also known as wetters or spreaders.

Waterlogging A condition in soil where all air spaces are filled (saturated) with water and oxygen is excluded.

Winter wash The application of a fungicide or insecticide to the stems and branches of dormant deciduous plants.

Wilt The partial or total collapse of a plant due to water loss or root damage.

Windrock The loosening of a plant's roots caused by wind.

Wound paint A paint or paste applied to cover a cut or damaged area on a plant, such as occurs when a branch is removed.

Wind-throw The uprooting of a tree by wind. Decay in the tree roots can make the tree unstable and, therefore, susceptible to wind damage.

Xylem The conductive tissue under bark that takes water and nutrients up a stem.

index

acknowledgements

A–Z Botanical Collection 11 top, 83 top /Anthony Cooper 80 top /Brian Gadsby 5 centre, 28–29, 30–31, 32–33, 34–35 /Geoff Kidd 36–37, 38–39, 40–41, 42–43, 55 centre, 92 bottom /Richard Marpole 5 right, 29 right, 31 right, 33 right, 35 right /Mrs W. Monks 115 centre /Steven Owens 81 top /Steve Taylor 1, 3

Emap Gardening Picture Library 58 top, 65 bottom, 72 top, 105 top, 109 bottom

Garden & Wildlife Matters 99 top, 117 top

Octopus Publishing Group Limited 76 /Michael Boys 7, 53 /Andrew Lawson 102 /Peter Myers 86, 112 /George Wright 66

Holt Studios International /Richard Anthony 90 bottom /Andy Burridge 95 centre /Nigel Cattlin 5 left, 5 centre left, 5 centre right, 9 bottom, 11 bottom, 15 top, 15 bottom, 17 top, 19, 21 top, 21 bottom, 23 top, 23 bottom, 25, 28 left, 28 centre, 29 centre, 30 left, 30 centre, 31 centre, 32 left, 32 centre, 33 centre, 34 left, 34 centre, 35 centre, 36 left, 36 centre, 37 right, 38 left, 38 centre, 39 right, 40 left, 40 centre, 41 right, 42 left, 42 centre, 43 right, 44 centre, 44–45, 45 right, 46 centre, 46–47, 47 right, 48 centre, 48–49, 49 right, 54 top, 55 top, 56 top, 56 bottom, 57 top, 57 bottom, 58 centre, 58 bottom, 59 top, 59 centre, 60 bottom, 60 top, 61 top, 61 centre, 61 bottom, 62 top, 63 centre, 63 bottom, 64 top, 64 bottom, 65 top, 65 centre, 68 top, 68 bottom, 69 bottom, 70 top, 70 centre, 70 bottom, 71 top, 71 bottom, 72 centre, 73 top, 73 centre, 73 bottom, 74 top, 74 centre, 75 top, 78 top, 78 bottom, 79 top, 79 centre, 81 bottom, 82 top, 82 bottom, 83 centre, 83 bottom, 84 top, 88 top, 88 bottom, 89 top, 89 bottom, 90 top, 91 top, 91 centre, 92 top, 92 centre, 93 top, 93 bottom, 95 bottom, 96 top, 96 centre, 96 bottom, 97 top, 98 top, 98 bottom, 99 bottom, 100 top, 100 bottom, 101 top, 101 bottom, 104 top, 104 bottom, 106 top, 106 bottom, 107 bottom, 108 top, 108 bottom, 109 top, 110 bottom, 111 bottom, 114 top, 114 bottom, 115 top, 116 top, 116 bottom, 117 bottom, 118 top, 118 bottom, 119 top, 119 bottom /Roy Groom 80 bottom /Andy Hibbert 95 top /Paul Hobson 9 top centre, 69 top /Andy Morant 44 left, 46 left, 48 left /Miss P. Peacock 37 centre, 39 centre, 41 centre, 43 centre /Inga Spence 109 /Peter Wilson 105 centre

Oxford Scientific Films /Harold Taylor 27

Photos Horticultural 17 bottom, 63 Top, 85 centre, 100 centre, 111 top, 115 bottom

Science Photo Library /Astrid & Hans-Frieder Michler 91 bottom

Harry Smith Collection 13 top, 13 bottom, 45 centre, 47 centre, 49 centre, 54 bottom, 55 bottom, 59 bottom, 62 bottom, 69 centre, 74 bottom, 75 bottom, 79 bottom, 81 centre, 84 bottom, 85 top, 85 bottom, 94 top, 94 bottom, 97 bottom, 107 top, 107 centre, 110 top

Sven Hellqvist 105 bottom

Executive Editor Sarah Ford
Managing Editor Clare Churly
Executive Art Editor Peter Burt
Designer Les Needham
Production Controller Ian Paton
Picture Researcher Christine Junemann
Illustrator Amanda Patton